TOWARD THE LIGHT

Toward the Light

Cardinal Carlo Martini
ON ADVENT AND CHRISTMAS

Carlo M. Martini
Edited by Sergio Reseghetti
Translated by Demetrio S. Yocum

Paulist Press
New York / Mahwah, NJ

The Scripture quotations contained herein are from the New Revised Standard Version: Catholic Edition, Copyright © 1989 and 1993, by the Division of Christian Education of the National Council of the Churches of Christ in the United States of America. Used by permission. All rights reserved.

Interior image by Christos Georghiou / Shutterstock.com
Cover image: Alfredo Dagli Orti / The Art Archive at Art Resource, NY
Cover and book design by Lynn Else

Translation Copyright © 2015 by Paulist Press. Translated from Italian by Demetrio S. Yocum.

Originally published by Edizioni San Paolo, s.r.l.—Cinisello Balsamo (Milan) as *Verso la luce: Reflessioni sul Natale.* Copyright © 2013 by Edizioni San Paolo, s.r.l.—Cinisello Balsamo (Milan)

Library of Congress Cataloging-in-Publication Data

Martini, Carlo Maria, 1927–2012.
    [Verso la luce. English]
    Toward the light : Cardinal Carlo Martini on advent and Christmas / Cardinal Carlo M. Martini ; edited by Sergio Reseghetti.
        pages cm
    ISBN 978-0-8091-4942-1 (paperback) — ISBN 978-1-58768-533-0 (e-book)
    1. Advent—Meditations. 2. Christmas—Meditations. I. Reseghetti, Sergio, editor. II. Title.
    BV40.M38313 2015
    242`.33—dc23

                                                                            2015010777

ISBN 978-0-8091-4942-1 (paperback)
ISBN 978-1-58768-533-0 (e-book)

Published by Paulist Press
997 Macarthur Boulevard
Mahwah, New Jersey 07430

www.paulistpress.com

Printed and bound in the
United States of America

Contents

Introduction vii

1. The Origins of Christmas 1

2. In Darkness, a Great Light 9

3. A Hymn of Joy 21

4. God's Initiative 31

5. Acceptance and Rejection 39

6. You Will Find a Child in the
   Poverty of a Stable 67

7. Renouncing Impiety and
   Worldly Passions 79

8. This Grace of Salvation Is for All 89

9. The Happiest Wish 99

10. The Beginning of All Our Beginnings 111

11. God with Us 117

Introduction

As bishop, Cardinal Martini was particularly fond of the Feast of the Epiphany. In fact, on that day he also celebrated the anniversary of his episcopal ordination or, as St. Ambrose used to call it, his episcopal *dies natalis*, his "birthday" as bishop. To put it another way, it marked the beginning of his work of service to the Gospel and to the unity of humankind as well as of his dedication to the announcement of God's mercy for all humanity manifested in the person of Christ Jesus.

In particular, as archbishop of Milan, Cardinal Martini had a very clear idea of the fact that our experience of the events that shape the world is based on the understanding we have of ourselves and our personal mission, just as St. Paul, writing to the Ephesians, cited the ministry of God's grace that was "given me for you" (Eph 3:2). Indeed, it is only based on the understanding that each of us has of ourselves and of our personal missions the ability to participate actively and directly in the affairs of society at large.

Regarding this, Cardinal Martini used to recall a definition very dear to him that was coined by Pope John Paul II: the episcopate is a sacrament "on the road." It is a sacrament that leads a man to leave behind his personal world to walk among many other men and women, a sacrament that expresses the vocation of the Church to meet all human beings wherever they may be, to go and look for them, and cross their paths. The bishop is precisely the one who encourages and inspires the journeys of those who seek God in the darkness of the world. It is in this sense that the pope called the episcopate a sacrament "on the road," the sacrament that enables the bishops to cross the paths of every human being and help each one of them in their search for God. In addition, from the notion of the episcopate as a gift, as well as from John Paul II's definition of the episcopate as sacrament "en route," Cardinal Martini gradually became aware not only of his "insignificant" (as he liked to say) personal destiny and of his being on a journey with the much larger and more important destinies of the faithful of the diocesan community of Milan, but also of having the responsibilities of the diocesan community of Milan toward the other churches and communities of Europe and the whole world.

As bishop, Cardinal Martini was also able to cross the paths of many other men and women through his preaching the Word of God, a task of which he was very fond. Among his many sermons and lectures, the ones that particularly stand out are those he prepared for the feasts dedicated to the manifestation of Christ, especially Christmas and the Epiphany.

Going through the numerous sermons that Cardinal Martini, as archbishop of Milan, dedicated to Christmas, one is struck by the great timeliness of certain words, no doubt because of their profound truth and for the considerable prophetic quality of the preacher himself. But even more so, it has to do with the recurrence of human history and the fact that humanity is always the same and, therefore, always in need of the same thing: that God come to each one of us in tenderness.

The paradox of Christmas is that in this tenderness of God is also expressed God's glory. In the words of St. Irenaeus of Lyons, in his work *Adversus haereses* (IV.20.7), "*Gloria Dei vivens homo,*" the glory of God is man fully alive. Who could better represent the pure act of living than a helpless infant? The glory of God is thus manifested in the Son who became man, who became a child at Christmas.

But there is also another amazing and paradoxical aspect of this poor infant who came into the world in a stable: all humanity must come to terms with him. Faced with the fact of Jesus, no one can remain indifferent. Every man and every woman has to choose whether to reject or welcome this shocking and ever-present event.

Finally, I would like to recall, as Cardinal Martini did in one of his homilies, the words spoken by another illustrious archbishop of Milan, Cardinal Montini, later Pope Paul VI, who in 1956 proclaimed to the assembly of the faithful gathered in the cathedral for the Feast of the Epiphany, "The coming of Christ gives rise to a spiritual drive in the world, a drive that will never end. No one can miss the invitation to contemplate the light of Christ; we only have to open our eyes, and just make the first steps to get closer to it. Those who yearn, will be rewarded. Those who reflect, will understand. Those who pray, will rejoice."

Sergio Reseghetti

1

The Origins of Christmas

The main Feast of early Christianity—and still the biggest celebration of the liturgical year—is not Christmas but Easter, the celebration of Jesus' death and resurrection. However, studies of ancient Easter sermons of the second and third centuries show that

Easter did not only celebrate Jesus' resurrection, but the salvific event as a whole, which is God's being for humanity and with humanity in Jesus. All this was in light of the entire history of salvation, the fact that God has always been with humanity from the beginning of history, in the history of the Jewish people, and then, in Jesus, for all people and forever.

Thus, the feast of Jesus' birth we celebrate on December 25 and call Christmas, which originated as a liturgical feast toward the end of the third century, also celebrated the whole mystery of Christ and not simply his historical nativity. It saw the celebration of Jesus' historical birth as the starting point of the whole mystery of Christ. The Feast of Christmas was also the result of intense and painful struggles to find the right vocabulary to express the mystery of Jesus as God and man.

After so many centuries, today we can ask ourselves the following questions: How can we communicate today the profound insights that emerged from and gave rise to the Feast of Christmas, the celebration of Jesus' birth, in the early centuries of Christianity? And how can we find access through the historical Feast of Christmas to the mystery of God?

First, when referring to Christ's birth, we must say that it is a specific and unequivocal event, one that belongs with all the other events of world history. Luke's Gospel tells the story of this birth. In particular, chapter 2 relates the facts concerning Jesus as they occurred under the Emperor Augustus Caesar. Chapter 1 tells of the events that occurred in the days of Herod, king of Judea. Chapter 3 recounts the events at the time of the Emperor Tiberius. Thus, as chapter 2 deals with the events concerning Jesus that happened under Emperor Augustus Caesar at the time of the census, we find ourselves between these other two events. The people featured in this story are, on the one hand, the emperor and, on the other, the newly-formed family of Joseph, a distant descendant of King David; Mary, his pregnant wife; their baby; and finally, the shepherds and angels. Heaven and earth, worldly powers and ordinary people, are drawn together in this scene to enlighten us on the significance of this particular birth:

> In those days a decree went out from Emperor Augustus that all the world should be registered. This was the first registration and was taken while Quirinius was governor of Syria. All went to their own towns to be registered. Joseph also went from the town of Nazareth in Galilee to Judea, to the city of David called Bethlehem, because he was descended from the house and family of

David. He went to be registered with Mary, to whom he was engaged and who was expecting a child. While they were there, the time came for her to deliver her child. And she gave birth to her firstborn son and wrapped him in bands of cloth, and laid him in a manger, because there was no place for them in the inn.

In that region there were shepherds living in the fields, keeping watch over their flock by night. Then an angel of the Lord stood before them, and the glory of the Lord shone around them, and they were terrified. But the angel said to them, "Do not be afraid; for see—I am bringing you good news of great joy for all the people: to you is born this day in the city of David a Savior, who is the Messiah, the Lord. This will be a sign for you: you will find a child wrapped in bands of cloth and lying in a manger." And suddenly there was with the angel a multitude of the heavenly host, praising God and saying:

"Glory to God in the highest heaven,
and on earth peace among those whom he favors!"

When the angels had left them and gone into heaven, the shepherds said to one another, "Let us go now to Bethlehem and see this thing that has taken place, which the

Lord has made known to us." So they went with haste and found Mary and Joseph, and the child lying in the manger. When they saw this, they made known what had been told them about this child; and all who heard it were amazed at what the shepherds told them. But Mary treasured all these words and pondered them in her heart. The shepherds returned, glorifying and praising God for all they had heard and seen, as it had been told them. (Luke 2:1–20)

Thus, we can say that Luke tells the story of Jesus' birth in two movements. In the first, we find the historical, human, visible coordinates, those common to all other similar events and births that occur, are occurring, and will occur in this world. The second conveys the special significance of this particular birth, which will be the focus of this book.

At the outset, the Gospel informs us of the historical and political context in which Jesus' birth took place, namely that of the Roman Empire at the time of its great expansion and unification under the Emperor Augustus Caesar, whose given name was Octavian Augustus. Augustus came to power in 29 BC, was proclaimed "Augustus"—the sovereign, the divine—in 27 BC, and reigned for many years until AD 14. Therefore, the political horizon of Jesus' birth and early life coincides with this great emperor whose name, deeds, and events are well attested to in all historical accounts.

Within this great political framework, we find one that is narrower, more local and administrative: that of Syria, where Quirinius was governor, and the Palestine of the time, where a census was imposed. Usually, in provinces subject to Rome, censuses occasioned rebellion, riots, and great turmoil because a census meant a province was no longer a merely symbolic possession of foreigners but a taxable one. Therefore, the population feared such measures. However, Luke's account does not give any hint of this probable dramatic social background at the time of this particular census. It is primarily an administrative, fiscal act, as are the censuses still carried out today after so many centuries.

Thus, we have a political situation, an administrative event, and in this context—narrowing the focus of our attention—a small, ancient city with a famous name: Bethlehem, famous as the city of origin of the great Davidic dynasty that had reigned in Israel. If we examine this large political picture more closely, this administrative event and this small town, we meet a family, a man and a woman, Joseph and Mary. Mary is worried and short of breath; she is pregnant and almost ready to give birth. Here we can observe again a series of facts that are common everywhere, especially when people are forced to migrate, when they are in distress and cannot find a dwelling place or new home. Even this young man and his pregnant wife cannot find shelter. Unable to find suitable lodging, the woman gives birth in the fields, under a roof found at the last moment, in a stable for animals.

This is the historical event so far. We could consider it a news story in that it has a very precise and simple political, contextual, administrative, geographic setting. It is nothing extraordinary, but it is a painful case of poverty and isolation: people who cannot find anyone willing to help in a moment of need. So far, the first part of this Gospel recounts a fact like so many others in this world: a birth, which unlike others, is in this poor and improvised context, a context of distress and loneliness, indicating lack of charity and hospitality of the people of that time toward those who came from far away.

This general historical picture points out that the significance of the event of Christmas and the mystery of Jesus is not only religious, but also social and political—even if God is revealed in humility, in the vulnerability of an indigent child. Here we also see in the

Gospel the members of Jesus' family: Joseph, of the house and family of David, who goes to Bethlehem to be registered with Mary, his pregnant wife, who gives birth to Jesus in a manger because there was no place at the inn. Thus, Luke puts the birth of Jesus well within the framework of universal history to show that human history is at the service of God's plan, and that even Caesar's order serves an extraordinary event: the birth of the Messiah.

2
In Darkness, a Great Light

"The people who walked in darkness / have seen a great light; / those who lived in a land of deep darkness— / on them light has shined." This is how the Prophet Isaiah presents the mystery of the revelation of God's grace among humanity at the beginning of chapter 9, read on Christmas Day in the Ambrosian Rite.* It is also how the Church presents the mystery of Christmas on the day of its celebration: a great light that shines in a land of deep darkness. Even the Gospel read during Mass on December 25, which describes the appearance of the angels to the shepherds, says, "…and the glory of the LORD shone around them." These words, "a great light" that shines "in a land of deep darkness," are not only very evocative, but also a metaphor for and symbol of many realities.

For the Prophet, who spoke to the men of his time, the "light" referred to the salvation that God would manifest in the sad situation of the people of Israel, a people who had no future, or better, whose future was haunted by spirits of war and death. The oracle of the Prophet Isaiah presupposes a situation similar to what many countries experience today, especially in the Middle East—"all the boots of the tramping warriors" (Isa 9:5) still resonate today throughout those countries. In the text of Isaiah, the historical reference was to the invasion of Israel by Assyria, then a great empire in northern Mesopotamia, located in an area that is now

---

* The Ambrosian Rite is a liturgical rite of the Western Church, named after St. Ambrose, bishop of Milan from 374 to 397, approved for use primarily in the Archdiocese of Milan. It has its own lectionary or cycle of Mass readings that differs from that used in the more familiar Roman Rite. Cardinal Martini will refer to it throughout the book.—Ed.

comprised of parts of Iraq, Syria, and Turkey. From there, Assyrian armies had already advanced to the territory of Israel, had occupied the Golan Heights, and entered into Galilee: Jerusalem was clearly threatened.

In the context of the liturgy, which announces these words to all men and women, the Prophet is alluding to God's light that shines in the darkness of our sin, in that state of gloom in which we lie, which prevents us from knowing God, ourselves, and our future.

Thus, a deep darkness covers the land and obscures the nations: this "darkness" is the fear of believing, of relying on the love of God the Father; this shadow is that of our rat races that prevent us from recognizing our neighbors. If we want to find an expression that better conveys to us today the meaning of this darkness, what is meant by this situation of obscurity in our present moment, I think we could aptly compare it, among other things, to a situation of distrust and lack of faith: a generalized distrust that meanders almost everywhere.

Behind this word used by the Scriptures to define the situation of human sin are many aspects that are part of our daily experience: our fear of each other; the worries and fears of living in big cities, of being attacked and assaulted; the fear of being cheated; and the fear that someone smarter than us might enter into our lives and mess with our business. In addition, if we look at the bigger picture, there is the fear of the future that, for some, is connected with the fear of living and, for others, of giving life. This fear and distrust that constitute our situation of darkness can also become, or be expressed, as fear of God, that same fear that Adam was the first to feel in the Garden of Eden after his crime; the fear of a God who condemns us, or exposes our selfishness and our sin.

Therefore, the people are in a deep darkness, as those who walk blindfolded and do not know where to go, where to put their feet, where to turn, without hope. At precisely this moment the announcement is made: "The people who walked in darkness / have seen a great light; / those who lived in a land of deep darkness [i.e., occupied, threatened, oppressed by the enemy]— / on them light has shined" (Isa 9:2).

In the midst of this darkness that we all know well, the Prophet Isaiah senses something and shouts with emotion that in Jerusalem the light will soon appear: "Arise, shine; for your light has come, / and the glory of the LORD has risen upon you" (Isa 60:1). Attracted by this mysterious light that is Christ, the people walk toward Jerusalem. This holy city, a symbol of Jesus and the Messiah, joyfully contemplates the universal pilgrimage of its scattered children converging from every part of the earth to proclaim the glory of the Lord, to serve and worship God, to live happily as brothers and sisters in peace, without rivalry and exploitation.

As mentioned above, in addition to chapter 9, in the Ambrosian Rite, there is another reading from the Book of the Prophet Isaiah during the Christmas season. Chapter 60, read during the celebration of the Epiphany, is an eschatological poem—meaning that it deals with the last things and the ultimate destiny of humanity— also dominated by the image of the light and could be titled "Ode to the Coming Light" or "Ode to the Light of Nations." This song begins with the exhortation, "Arise, shine"; in the original Hebrew text *shine* corresponds to *auri*, that is "be radiant," "be bright":

Arise, shine; for your light has come,
    and the glory of the LORD has risen upon you.
For darkness shall cover the earth,
    and thick darkness the peoples;
but the LORD will arise upon you,
    and his glory will appear over you.
Nations shall come to your light,
    and kings to the brightness of your dawn.

Lift up your eyes and look around;
  they all gather together, they come to you.
                                        (Isa 60:1–4)

So what is the reason for the Prophet Isaiah's exhortation to "shine," to "be bright"? The pattern is repeated four times: "shine; for your light has come," because "the glory of the LORD has risen upon you"; "the LORD will arise upon you," and "his glory will appear over you." The reason for this exhortation to "shine" is the Lord's coming: God, the Lord, is the source of light.

After this exhortation to shine and after explaining the reasons to be bright comes the revelation of the effects of this radiance: "Nations shall come to your light, / and kings to the brightness of your dawn." The people walk by the light while everywhere around there is deep darkness.

In this exhortation to shine and become bright, we can therefore see described, supported, and exemplified in its effects a historical process that has four phases: first, we have darkness and obscurity; second, the light of the coming Lord; third, the moment of shining and becoming bright by the light; and, finally, the journey of the people toward this light. Throughout both this reading of the Epiphany and the remainder of chapter 60, Isaiah describes the journey, the procession of the people toward this light. His description is still preceded by an exhortation: "Lift up your eyes and look around." Then, for the rest of the chapter, he describes this great procession of people.

This passage from chapter 60 of the Book of Isaiah not only raises some questions, but offers some insights as well. First, we wonder: who is this "you" who is called here to shine, to be bright, and to whom the whole song is addressed. The answer lies in verse three: "Nations shall come to your light, and kings to the brightness of your dawn": this "you" is Jerusalem. But not the Jerusalem in its miserable condition at the time when Isaiah proclaimed his prophecy; rather, Jerusalem seen in its future fulfillment: the Jerusalem that we hope and long for; the one that will be more glorious than in the days of David, more beautiful than the one rebuilt after the Babylonian captivity.

So what is this event of light? This coming and shining of the Lord is the same Lord who comes to man, the coming of the kingdom of God, Jesus' incarnation. On Christmas Eve, we proclaim the Prologue of John's Gospel in the Ambrosian Rite: "The light shines in the darkness, and the darkness did not overcome it....The true light, which enlightens everyone, was coming into the world" (John 1:5, 9).

This coming of Jesus, this event of incarnation, is made present, shown, and manifested (*epiphany* means precisely "manifestation") in many other events of Jesus' life that are recalled in the liturgy of the Epiphany. First, Jesus' manifestation to the Magi, as reported in the Gospel according to Matthew, in which we can read our call to faith; then, other manifestations of Jesus' public life such as his baptism in the Jordan, with the voice from heaven calling him "Son," in which we can read our own baptism that makes us children of God; finally, the water changed into wine at Cana, and the multiplication of the loaves that we can interpret as the wine and bread of the Eucharist. Thus, Jesus' manifestation continues in the sacraments and reaches us in the eucharistic celebration.

All these events, which are remembered on the Feast of the Epiphany, show the pervasive and transforming power of this light that has come into the world and illuminates the city of the children of God. This city, illuminated by the light of the Lord, is therefore the community of God's kingdom, the assembly of those who accept the teachings of Jesus as precepts of life and rely on his forgiveness and grace. It is the community of the kingdom seen in its eternal fullness, yet already inaugurated here on earth in the present. Therefore, the exhortation "shine" is addressed to all of us.

The second question has to do with this procession of the nations toward the light. This represents the conversion that takes place in the world starting from the light of God's kingdom and from the light that radiates from the community that lives the values of God's kingdom. It also represents the conversion that will culminate in the eternal meeting of all peoples in God. All that the Prophet says has already begun in the mystery of Bethlehem and the Magi. In the deep darkness, the light has come into the world, reaching remote places, so that the Magi have walked toward the brightness of God's glory bringing gold, frankincense, and myrrh, and proclaiming the glories of the Lord.

This light, then, has already appeared, but is still ahead of us: it is the future of God that attracts all human history, moment by moment. Therefore, this mystery takes place whenever the Holy Spirit illuminates with the light of Christ some human reality, individual existence, family, society, or community until it reaches eternal fullness.

All this, and the same message of the Prophet Isaiah, invite us to consider with a confident outlook the historical process that humanity is experiencing. In fact, we can find in its process the same phases seen in the biblical text: first of all, the moment of deep darkness, not only physical but also cultural and spiritual, which no doubt is present in our times. In this regard, a few verses before chapter 60, the Prophet Isaiah declared, "We wait for light, and lo! there is darkness; / and for brightness, but we walk in gloom. / We grope like the blind along a wall, / groping like those who have no eyes; / we stumble at noon as in the twilight" (59:9–10). There is no lack of the same darkness, blindness, and confusion that the Prophet Isaiah encountered, experienced, and foresaw. But in this darkness, says the Prophet, the Lord comes. The Lord is coming now, today, in his Word, in the Eucharist, and in the grace of the Holy Spirit. He comes, and will come, to illuminate anyone who is willing to welcome the light. We are among those who want to be illuminated, those who want to take as true the meaning of life that Jesus transmits with his life and words, beginning with the humility and simplicity of Bethlehem. Therefore, the exhortation "shine" applies to us, our Church, our families, and each one of our lives. "Arise, shine!"

The readings from the Prophet Isaiah in the liturgy during the Christmas season speak therefore of light: "The people who walked in darkness / have seen a great light" (Isa 9:2); this is the light of God that brings peace and freedom in a world marked by conflict, violence, and oppression. But in that night, in the deep darkness in which the people walked, what made possible the coming of the light that turned sadness into joy? Of course, Isaiah alludes here to the historical liberation from the oppression of the Assyrian empire and its army's flight from Jerusalem. However, Isaiah, as Prophet of God's people and of future times, also refers here to that moment, to that time in which any type of army and threat of war will disappear. In other words, Isaiah is foretelling the jubilation of the people for the birth of the one who will be the Prince of Peace, the Everlasting Father, the Wonderful Counselor of peace and justice. Therefore, there is no comparison between our darkness and Jesus' great light. We can also look at the whole of human history as decided by this birth. If, in disbelief, we ask the Prophet Isaiah, "But how can this be? How will it be possible in a world increasingly torn by conflicts and fears of war?" Isaiah will reply, once again, "The zeal of the LORD of hosts will do this" (Isa 9:7).

Thus, we can find in the words of the Prophet Isaiah the earliest core of the Christmas message.

3
A Hymn of Joy

The light announced by the Scriptures is full of a genuine and deeply human joy, "as with joy at the harvest, / as people exult when dividing plunder" (Isa 9:3): the Lord breaks the burden of the yoke across the shoulders. It is no wonder that the Prophet Isaiah, in awe as he faces the light that shines in the darkness and, contemplating this vision, exclaims to God, "You have multiplied the nation, / you have increased its joy" (Isa 9:3); and soon after he explains the reason for this joy: "For the yoke of their burden/ …you have broken…. / For a child has been born for us, / a son given to us; / authority rests upon his shoulders; and he is named / …Prince of Peace. / …and there shall be endless peace / for the throne of David and his kingdom" (Isa 9:4–7).

Christmas is the day of joy par excellence and, once again, the reason for this joy is proclaimed by the angel to the shepherds in Luke's Gospel that is read every December 25 in the Ambrosian Rite: "To you is born this day in the city of David a Savior, who is the Messiah, the Lord" (Luke 2:11); and previously the angel had said, "I am bringing you good news of great joy for all the people" (2:10) because God's salvation is for everyone, without exception.

But we all must ask ourselves what kind of salvation humanity needs, and who this Savior really is. Once again, we can find the answer in reading from the Prophet Isaiah: "The people who walked in darkness / have seen a great light; / those who lived in a land of deep darkness— / on them light has shined" (Isa 9:2). The salvation that we all need is to be freed from the darkness that surrounds us and makes us uneasy, worried, troubled, and fearful. The Prophet Isaiah speaks of war and the enemy's oppression, but many other forms of darkness oppress us all. Yet, in the darkness, a symbol of chaos and death, suddenly, almost miraculously, a light shines—a great light that fills the people with joy and gladness. This light is a child sent from God, a child who carries the authority on his shoulders and is called "Wonderful Counsellor, Mighty God, / Everlasting Father, Prince of Peace" (Isa 9:6). Thus, in this passage, Isaiah proclaims the coming of the Savior, who is for us a source of joy.

Great joy is therefore the first and foremost trait of Christmas; a great joy—Isaiah says—as the joy of exultation in the days of victory, as when dividing plunder; a proclaimed, ineffable joy; a joy not only of a few, but of all people; and the root of this joy is found in the words of the Gospel: "To you is born this day in the city of David a Savior, who is the Messiah, the Lord" (Luke 2:11); a child, like the one foretold by Isaiah, whose marvelous titles, include "Savior," "Christ," and "Lord." This means that the nations, humanity, and history have finally found their point of reference, the only one who saves and who frees from anxiety, fear, evil, war, hatred, and death. Therefore, humanity's hope that life is meaningful and more beautiful than the single events that we experience—especially if we consider the painful ones that continually dot the sky of our existence—comes true. It is wonderful to be alive, to look to the future, and to be hopeful because there is a Savior, Christ the Lord, in whom all our hope becomes, and will become, reality. We are no longer lost and alone; there is someone who guides us, who takes care of us and this is Jesus Christ, the *Messiah*, which means "sent by God": God has appointed him to save humanity.

The message of Christmas is about life, joy, creativity, hope, friendship, and impetuous love that move history and the human experience. It is a message of great joy that changes the monotony and uniformity of life while giving it meaning and hope, thus transforming it from within.

The same Christmas liturgy, from the first to the third reading, is a hymn of joy, an invitation to be joyful, for the announcement of the angel to us is "Do not be afraid; for see—I am bringing you good news of great joy…to you is born this day…a Savior" (Luke 2:10–11).This is how the liturgy wishes us "Merry Christmas"; it does so in a biblical, theological, liturgical form, but also in one that we can then translate into these simple words of salutation that we warmly exchange with one another on Christmas Day.

As the Scriptures teach us, this great joy of God's great love for humanity that changes history forever is announced to some shepherds, who in those days were considered the lowest social class. And yet, they are the ones who first hear the voice of the heavenly host praising God, and singing, "Glory to God in the highest heaven, / and on earth peace among those whom he favors!" (Luke 2:14). "Glory to God in the highest" is also the chant that is intoned at the eucharistic celebration on Sundays, solemnities, and feasts; it is a joyful contemplation and adoration of God's great name and creative and redemptive love, as well as of the trinitarian mystery.

All the main characters in the gospel story of Jesus' birth are partakers of this joy: the angels, the shepherds, and the Magi. In fact, the evangelist Matthew writes that after their stay in Jerusalem, where Herod causes a setback on their journey, the Magi, now guided not only by the star but also by the Scriptures, resume their journey, and when they see the star stop, they feel a great joy. Matthew does not reveal their previous emotional state, but reporting this joy, now that they are close to their goal, he suggests that at the outset of their journey, they felt some apprehension and struggle. The same happens to us: what we must take from this passage is that after apprehension and struggle we will feel joy.

The joy felt by the protagonists of that holy night of two thousand years ago is now announced to all humanity. And in this regard, I recall a personal experience from a Christmas morning, while celebrating the Eucharist behind the prison bars of Opera.* As I had the good fortune to experience, many people, even those who live in such a tragic situation, are inundated with the emotions and the joy of Christmas, knowing that true freedom is at hand; the same joy that we saw in the Prophet Isaiah when announcing the birth of a child ("a child has been born for us"), who is the sign of a new world.

The Book of the Prophet Isaiah, which we read during the celebration of Christmas Eve in the Ambrosian Rite, announces the return of the exiles to Jerusalem. Therefore, we also are invited to sing for joy with the Prophet, as the watchmen on the walls of the holy city, because the Lord comes to open our eyes with his light, warm our hearts with his love, and remove our interior and exterior miseries.

There is another passage in the Book of the Prophet Isaiah that can be read as a prelude to the joy of

---

* Opera, near Milan, is a large, high-security prison in Italy.—Ed.

Christmas, and this is in the form of a song. In chapter 54, right after the last of the Servant Songs, Isaiah breaks into a song of joy: "Sing, O barren one who did not bear; / burst into song and shout, / you who have not been in labor! / For the children of the desolate woman will be more / than the children of her that is married, says the LORD" (v. 1). This whole section is pervaded by the triumphant exultation of one who is thought to be defeated and is instead proclaimed victorious. The defeated is represented here as a barren and abandoned woman. In this image, we can see Jerusalem, defeated and humiliated but to whom victory is promised. We can see the persecuted and marginalized Church still confiding in the Lord. Finally, we can see each one of us who believed in the gospel and made a final, irrevocable decision (that is, trusting in God alone and for this reason, sometimes feeling alone and abandoned), and is therefore inwardly comforted by these promises. This page from Isaiah therefore describes the joy of Christmas, of the God-among-us who enters into our humility to let us rejoice in God's glory. It also presents the self-contained fertility of the Virgin Mary, who will give birth to the Word, the Son of God.

Isaiah here is also wondering how there could be such a joyful exultation. The answer is because God loves us: "For the mountains may depart / and the hills be removed, / but my steadfast love shall not depart from you, / and my covenant of peace shall not be removed, / says the LORD, who has compassion on you" (Isa 54:10).

This song, by drawing our attention to the Old Testament imagery, presents even more tangibly the fullness and joy of a human life and a human experience that rely only on the Lord, and which are fully invested in God; the fullness and joy of a spiritual life dedicated to the service of God; the fullness and joy that we may find in human experience in general, as well as in cultural and intellectual experiences when they participate in this faith in the power of the Lord. In short, we could say that this page from Isaiah shows the fullness and joy of Christianity lived in all aspects of life.

This is precisely the secret of Christian life and its joy. A secret that is about understanding that with the coming of Jesus in the world, nothing has changed— in a certain sense—regarding external events: we still laugh and cry; we get sick or well; we fight or win, and then die; life goes on just as it was before Jesus' coming. But for those who welcome the angel's message, the meaning of each single event changes, as do the horizon and the perspective in which it occurs, and the inner strength with which it is lived. Thus, everything changes. This transformation is similar to what happens in mathematics: in place of a negative sign before the number, there is now a positive one. Instead of a "minus," there is a "plus": the number seems the same, but its value has completely changed.

Similarly, once we welcome Jesus into our hearts, everything changes: life, history, and eternity. Everything is new, everything can acquire a new meaning, everything has a meaning; every form of pain is now infused with hope, and every joy with moderation and cheerfulness; every activity is experienced as something that truly builds, either here or later, that house in which we will dwell one day.

It is essential to always remember that the joy of Christmas is not only related to a historical event that took place in Bethlehem two thousand years ago, but is linked to the here and now of God's salvation; a here and now that includes all times: past, present, and future. This joy fills the holy night in which the whole event is celebrated, a joy that will culminate and reach its full expression on Easter morning. In effect, Christmas Eve should not be considered a single event, but rather the starting point of our journey of redemption and the beginning of the concrete revelation of God's falling in love with us, which is ultimately expressed in an extreme and extraordinary manner in Jesus' death and resurrection, that is, at Easter. It comes as no surprise then that in the ancient liturgies—and even nowadays, for example, in the Spanish language—Christmas is defined as the "Easter of birth," in correspondence with the "Easter of resurrection."

In conclusion, I would like to recall Pope John Paul II's words, commenting on the verse of Isaiah, "Arise, shine; / for your light has come" (60:1), proclaimed in his homily for the Feast of the Epiphany in 2001: "Yet we cannot but be filled with joy, with that inner joy to which the Prophet calls us, a joy rich in thanksgiving and praise, because it is based on our awareness of the gifts received and our certainty of Christ's enduring love."* This joy has its source in the fact that the liturgy celebrates the manifestation of Jesus to all humanity, which is called, through him, to the intimacy of a life with God.

---

* Closing of the Holy Door: Homily of Pope John Paul II. Solemnity of the Epiphany, Saturday, January 6, 2001, http://www.vatican.va/liturgy_seasons/christmas/documents/hf_jp-ii_hom_20010106_closing_en.html.

4

God's Initiative

Among many other things, in the dynamics of the Christmas event, God's approach toward humanity emerges powerfully. God, the infinite, the eternal, who is above all created things, has taken care of the last born of creation—that is, the human creature—has leaned toward it, and decided to interact with it. Better still, God has joined humanity in such an extraordinary and astonishing way as to generate on earth a human being, Jesus, who has in himself the unattainable fullness of God's divinity. But there is even more: this coming of God to humanity did not occur in a universe that man has respected and guarded, making it habitable and attractive, but in an environment and world degraded by the exploitation that humanity has inflicted on creation and one another, in a history torn by cruelty and war, among a corrupt and fallen humanity. Thus, in God there is a loving and merciful inclination toward us creatures that is so great that it wants to be part not only of our happy events, but also of our painful stories, and to support and bring each man and woman to God's truth, to the filial dialogue with the Creator and Father of all beings.

It is precisely through the Christmas event that God's inclination and propensity for humanity are unequivocally revealed, a propensity that goes so far as to become, in Jesus, a partaker of our history of suffering, so that this history of ours may become, through Jesus, a history of salvation.

From the contemplation of this mystery, of the mystery that is this child, the Son of God born for us, we can draw a fundamental conclusion: the basis of every human search for God is that God is love pouring out toward humanity, and that God seeks us first. Therefore, the emphasis is on God's initiative; it is God who gives himself to humankind through signs, events, and epiphanies. The precise meaning of *epiphany* is "manifestation of God."

These divine epiphanies, or manifestations, are many, and the liturgy of the Feast of the Epiphany, which is closely linked to that of Christmas, recalls four in particular: the star followed by the Magi; the baptism in the Jordan; the water changed into wine at the wedding at Cana; and the multiplication of the loaves and fishes. These events, these epiphanies, are signs, as sung in the preface that opens the Eucharistic prayer for the Epiphany, of the divine will to give to us the knowledge of God's glory in Jesus. Like Christmas, the Feast of the Epiphany teaches us many things. It tells us that we are not the first to seek God, but it is God who first seeks us—and does so tirelessly. It tells us that God directs the path of every man and every woman on earth toward the meeting with God's Son Jesus, who draws all humanity to himself. If we all really believed that God loved us infinitely and passionately, wars, violence, and conflicts would disappear from the face of the earth and a civilization of peace and harmony would blossom like a flower.

Thus, in all its symbols, the Feast of the Epiphany celebrates the primacy of God's initiative of salvation and reminds all of us "in the beginning was the Word," as stated in the Prologue of John's Gospel. In other words, in the beginning, we do not find humanity in search of God, or trying to approach God; rather, in the beginning, there is God who is made manifest, who speaks and is made known through visible signs, accessible to the mind and heart, and who is in search of humanity. Therefore, the believer, who is the man or woman who achieves the fullness of self-consciousness, does not first ask at a specific moment, "What shall I do?" or "What must I say?" but "What is God saying? What is God saying to me? What is being revealed to me through the signs of God's will?" It is not the Magi themselves who take the initiative to set out, but it is the star that calls them, and after the star, the Scripture prophecies interpreted in Jerusalem tell them what they must do: it is the primacy of the Word, of God's initiative of salvation. Humanity becomes the ear listening to the Word of God, and by doing so, realizes itself and its life. In short, humanity becomes fully itself when it listens with full attention to God's Word manifested in Jesus.

Through the story of the Magi, the evangelist Matthew wants to reveal to us precisely that the pilgrimage of all people toward the Father becomes real with Jesus. To this universal message, Matthew adds another comforting word that helps us to understand that it is God who first searches for us to then teach us how to seek and find God. This search for humanity on God's part, this attraction and call are here expressed by the sign of the star: it is the symbol of our inner voice, the voice that comes from the Spirit of God. In fact, it is the Spirit of God who tirelessly knocks on the door of the human heart to open it to the revelation and guide it to the meeting with the Lord Jesus. The history of each one of us, the history of every man and woman on earth, is oriented toward the encounter with God in Christ. It is as if this voice had said to the Magi, "Get up, go, set out." It is, in effect, a voice that arouses in them the desire to set out; a voice that arouses the thirst for truth and the desire for the fullness of life that in turn set in motion a search that leads to living an authentic existence.

In the Ambrosian Rite, the second reading of the Christmas Mass confirms what we have observed earlier.

In fact, St. Paul writes in his Letter to Titus, "For the grace of God has appeared, bringing salvation to all" (Titus 2:11). Simply put, what appears is that attitude of benevolent and gratuitous tenderness with which God loves us first. In the face of the distrust of the world, the mutual fear that could attack and infect all human relationships, God trusts us, comes toward us, and shows us this divine trust by putting in our hands God's Son. As we know, a child lives completely on trust, relying on others, in self-abandonment, with a belief in others that knows no mistrust. God puts in our midst God's only Son, as a child, as an example of this trust, reliance, and belief in us. Hence, God shows confidence in us, trusts humanity, and relies on us to the point of giving what God holds most dearly: himself in the Son as a helpless child in our hands. In order to heal our suspicious and fearful hearts, God chooses the path of dialogue and trust. Jesus does not come among us with authority, but with kindness; he comes to reveal to us the benevolent, patient, and tender mercy of the Father.

At Christmas, the Word of God proclaims the simplest but most important message: we are not abandoned and alone in a world that came out of nothing or by chance, we are not tossed in a whirlwind of meaningless events. Rather, we are loved, loved by God. We are loved without limits—without any merit on our part.

This is the fundamental announcement that we must welcome with the simple joy of a child: we are loved just as we are, despite all our weaknesses, despite our deeply embedded sins; better still, *because of them*. In fact, God became man to save us from our sins and our mistakes; from our omissions, stupidity, and ignorance, as well as from our despair and cruelty. The Father who forgives us without limits is the one from whom everything is and on whom everything depends, to whom all tend and return.

Often, we Christians think that we must first be good and honest so that we can deserve to be loved by God. However, this is the wrong way of thinking. The revelation of Christmas night is there to confirm it to us: we need first to be loved by God and be assured of God's forgiving love in order to be able to become good and love God and our neighbors in return. The demand to be good first leads us to a dead end and puts us in a discouraging situation. We cannot genuinely love first; there is too much evidence of this in the great hatreds and conflicts we hear every day in the news, and also in the numerous pains we inflict on each other in everyday life, in our families, at work, in the reality of our quotidian experience. We can only love too little.

Instead, the wonderful gift of love that God gives us freely by loving us first provides us with the light, joy, and courage we need to walk and persevere even in the darkest moments, along with the confidence and daring to make the first step toward others, toward that mysterious gesture called forgiveness.

Thanks to Christmas, we Christians are ready to believe in the paschal mystery that God is the Father who loves us first, who communicates and offers himself to us in Jesus—even before any expectations on our part.

5
Acceptance and Rejection

To recognize the presence of a divine initiative in the Feast of Christmas means, accordingly, to grasp the existence of a divine purpose, of God's purpose—that is to say, precisely how God wants to intervene in history through a plan of love and salvation for humanity.

This exact word, *purpose*, also is found, albeit in a negative context, in Luke 7:30, regarding the Pharisees and the lawyers, who "rejected God's purpose for themselves." Jesus pronounces these words with sadness after speaking of John the Baptist, and referring to both groups because of their attitude toward the Baptist. However, these sad words (because they imply that humanity can also thwart God's plan, not only with regard to one's life but also to society) contain a profound seed of hope as well. First, they confirm, by the words of Jesus himself, that God has a purpose not only for the life of each one of us, but also for society and its institutions. Second, we can infer that, just as this purpose of God can be thwarted by the laziness, negligence, and stupidity of human beings, so it can be carried out, fulfilled, and brought to fruition with human collaboration through the mystery of God's grace and the attention of and cooperation with all those of good will. Thus, God has a purpose for each of us, one that embraces our lives and our social and collective endeavors.

To prepare ourselves and welcome God's purpose for us, so we do not repeat Jesus' lament about the Pharisees and lawyers in the Gospel passage just quoted, means for every Christian to ask the following questions: Exactly how, Lord, are you revealing in this precise moment your purpose of salvation for us? How can we, in today's trials, be part of this purpose of salvation without thwarting it? The assumption, therefore, is that there is a purpose of salvation for all times, for every social, public, cultural situation. There are no absolute times of decline, just as there are no times of absolute progress, but there is always God's time, the *kairòs*, the Lord's time in which each one of us must realize what we are called to do. This time of the Lord exists because there is also this divine purpose of reassurance, consolation, joy, and peace for all times, even the most difficult ones.

The purpose of God means that God, the Creator, the Lord, the Redeemer, the one who calls us, who lifts us up with great love, invites us to open our hearts and arms to the divine presence in this historical time.

If we take into account the page of the Gospel proclaimed in the Ambrosian Rite on Christmas Eve, we read that it speaks of the Word who is with the Father, of its creative action, of the gifts of life and light with which everything is enriched. Then we come to the dramatic contrast between those who refused the Word and those who welcomed it: "He came to what was his own, and his own people did not accept him. But to all who received him, who believed in his name, he gave power to become children of God" (John 1:11–12). Central to the Prologue of John's Gospel is the drama of human freedom. Therefore, this passage of the Gospel speaks of us also, in particular of the choices that our freedom is called to make. The Gospel, without wasting time to explain the processes with which freedom is realized, goes straight to the heart of the problem, to the serious question of human freedom, making it clear that freedom is either rejected or welcomed.

Rejection is expressed in these words: "The world came into being through him; yet the world did not know him. He came to what was his own, and his own people did not accept him" (John 1:10–11). Rejection generates evil. We complain so much of the evil that is in our lives and society; we turn our thoughts, with pain and indignation, to the many evils that afflict the world.

But we must also ask from where all this evil comes. Evil comes from refusing to accept others and even ourselves, from not paying attention to others, from failing to ask what exactly is that love we say we feel for others and that we casually express to others during the Christmas holidays.

If we had the courage and patience to examine the various gifts that we long for, which we wish for ourselves and for others at Christmas, we would discover that they always point beyond, to a life and a light that are the divine gifts we receive from Jesus who comes into the world. Thus, evil is the rejection of Christ, whereas good—that is, the free pursuit of what is good—is the welcoming of Christ.

Even Luke's Gospel, which is read during Christmas Mass in the Ambrosian Rite, insists on the theme of Jesus who did not find a place to be born and was put in a manger because there was no room for him elsewhere. Freedom is to welcome Christ and to be open to the path that his love creates, to reveal to humanity the true love that is within the Father's heart. Thus, Christmas means to make room for Jesus: to make room for Jesus within us, and to make room for others in us as well.

This statement of the mystery of humanity as freedom and welcoming could be expanded with many concrete examples, with many instances from everyday life. This "making room" for Jesus, which is the key to the salvation of humanity, can be contrasted, for example, with the impatience and carelessness with which, in our society, we sometimes relate to others, even with the members of our own families. How impatient, how unwelcoming we often are with our families, even during the holidays! How impatient we are on the path of friendship! How hasty, careless, and materialistic we are on the path of love! How many sins arise from this inability to accept patiently others as persons, from the rush to use people up and consume relationships! Further, the inability to "make room" can become even indifference to the countless cases of need, suffering, and social alienation that coexist with the luxury and waste in our lives. And this inability to "make room" for others ultimately depends on the inability to welcome in our hearts the attitudes of reflection, of silent contemplation of the mystery of God, the nativity scene, and the mystery of Christmas.

Christmas reorients us toward the infinite possibilities of salvation created for us by the coming of the Word of God in our history—if only we open our hearts. Christmas is about making room for the Lord who comes. This opportunity is offered to our freedom. It is up to us to reject or accept it.

These two possible attitudes toward the manifestation of God in the Christmas mystery are clearly exemplified in the Gospel story of Herod and the three Magi.

The second chapter of Matthew, from which is selected the Gospel for the Feast of the Epiphany in the Ambrosian Rite, presents one of the themes most strictly linked to the existence of humanity. We might call it the theme of "the two-ways," of the two attitudes toward Christ that are expressed from the very first lines of this passage by the characters who are the main protagonists of this chapter:

> In the time of King Herod, after Jesus was born in Bethlehem of Judea, wise men from the East came to Jerusalem, asking, "Where is the child who has been born king of the Jews? For we observed his star at its rising, and have come to pay him homage." When King Herod heard this, he was frightened, and all Jerusalem with him; and calling together all the chief priests and scribes of the people, he inquired of them where the Messiah was to be born. They told him, "In Bethlehem of Judea; for so it has been written by the prophet:
>
> 'And you, Bethlehem, in the land of Judah,
>   are by no means least among the rulers of
>   Judah;
> for from you shall come a ruler
>   who is to shepherd my people Israel.'"
>
> Then Herod secretly called for the wise men and learned from them the exact time

when the star had appeared. Then he sent them to Bethlehem, saying, "Go and search diligently for the child; and when you have found him, bring me word so that I may also go and pay him homage." When they had heard the king, they set out; and there, ahead of them, went the star that they had seen at its rising, until it stopped over the place where the child was. When they saw that the star had stopped, they were overwhelmed with joy. On entering the house, they saw the child with Mary his mother; and they knelt down and paid him homage. Then, opening their treasure chests, they offered him gifts of gold, frankincense, and myrrh. And having been warned in a dream not to return to Herod, they left for their own country by another road. (Matt 2:1–12)

Thus, on one side of Jesus, the center of the whole narrative, there are the Magi, on the other, Herod. The Magi represent the search for and welcoming of God, while Herod epitomizes rejection, denial, and suppression. These two fundamental forces stir the human heart: acceptance and rejection. They are also the two realities that regulate our entire daily existence: to welcome or reject the gift of God. The liturgy of the

Epiphany recalls this universal symbolism of humanity's journey toward God.

This feast, therefore, celebrates the early and different manifestations of Jesus. At the same time, it recalls humanity's responses to these manifestations; in this sense, the Epiphany is our yes, better still, the yes of all believing humanity to the encounter with Christ, who was born and appeared in Bethlehem.

The Magi are those who hear the call and are led by the star toward the revelation, toward Jerusalem, where the scribes, the custodians of the Scriptures, will indicate where the King of the Jews is born and where the child that the Magi want to worship can be found.

But if the Magi are led by the star, Herod and the inhabitants of the city are afraid, and prefer not to be troubled in their consciences, and so they close themselves, refuse to listen to the voice, and refuse any type of news. Even the lawyers, being questioned, know how to give an accurate answer to the question about the Messiah's birthplace, but do not listen to their hearts, thus reducing the truth to an abstract formula that cannot change the fate of humanity.

Instead, the Magi believe in the Word written through the Prophet, and resuming the journey, set off for Bethlehem, led once again by the voice of their inner guide confirmed by the Scriptures. This is why, as the Gospel says, they are full of joy. They are overwhelmed by that joy typical of anyone who experiences a deep spiritual experience, the joy of those who finally see the light, the way, the life, the truth that is Jesus. The Magi prostrate themselves to worship the Child Jesus, whose beauty quenches their thirst for love and salvation, and they offer him everything they are and everything they have contemplated in Jesus, who is the great gift of God. In the story of the Magi, we can grasp the teaching that faith is both a gift and a conquest, a search that never ends.

Matthew's account of the story of the Magi is, therefore, a dramatic and provocative narrative founded on oppositions between the opening of the heart and eyes and the closing of the heart and mind. It is a story that puts side by side the attitude of the Magi and that of Herod, and with Herod's, that of the city and its cultural and religious representatives.

All those involved are determined to find out where exactly the expected Messiah was born, but they all are motivated by contrasting intentions. The Magi want to worship the Child Jesus and offer their gifts. The others want to know where he is because they fear this Messiah; they are afraid of him either because they see him as a pesky competitor, or as someone who will eventually wreck their plans and schemes for power.

Therefore, let us first contemplate the positive element, the light. The Magi symbolize the pilgrimage of humanity toward the encounter with the Lord. They also represent that great global pilgrimage or procession of generations and cultures that seek, each one on one's own or with others, to decipher the arduous and fascinating boundaries of existence.

God spoke to the hearts of some of these men seeking God; God spoke to the hearts of the Magi through the star that accompanied them on the long and hazardous journey from the Far East to Jerusalem. Once they arrive, the star disappears, then it returns to shine and guide them again to the house in which they find the Child Jesus with his mother. At that moment, as the Gospel says, "they were overwhelmed with joy" (Matt 2:10), recalling the joy of the apostles at the resurrection of Jesus described in John 20:20, "Then the disciples rejoiced when they saw the Lord," and also in Luke 24:41, "While in their joy they were disbelieving and still wondering," and 24:52, "and returned to Jerusalem with great joy."

Undoubtedly, this joy that the three Magi from the East felt came after much anxiety, darkness, fears, hardships, and struggles. Nevertheless, we are always struck by their loving docility and obedience. Even though they belong to a pagan people, they still rely on the star as a messianic sign. They let themselves be led by the Word of God; they prostrate themselves in humility and simplicity to worship Jesus, recognizing in him the King, the Lord, the Savior, the light of the world.

Not only the Magi, but each man and woman on earth is asked to let go in self-abandonment. We are urged to trust in someone who is guiding us in our lives, to push ourselves to venture a bit further than what our rational and calculating minds allow us to see. This is ultimately the Magi's role in the story.

On the other hand, their search for the child's birthplace troubles Herod. It becomes a matter of concern in the city, and puts the chief priests and the scribes on their guard. Herod fears being ousted by this new kind of king; the people, accustomed to a certain type of dictatorship, are afraid that some inconvenient change might occur; the chief priests and the scribes, who are also familiar with and know how to interpret the Scriptures, are fearful of events that might happen in the future.

Therefore, we can see the drama of Jesus' final rejection anticipated here, followed by his physical destruction. The suspicion toward his authority, which begins to surface here, will only continue to grow—in Jerusalem, in Herod, in the people and priests. This mistrust will accompany Jesus' every gesture and word, ultimately becoming the main accusation that will bring him to death on the cross, "He has claimed to be king."

Even today many fear Jesus. We are afraid of his uniqueness and singularity. We are afraid of Peter's declaration, when in Acts 4:12 he says, "There is salvation in no one else, for there is no other name under heaven given among mortals by which we must be saved." Today there is the tendency to see in this statement a manifestation of arrogance or religious colonialism, instead of seeing how Jesus, in his frailty, weakness, gentleness, and sweetness, is revealing the true path to peace.

Unfortunately, even today it is possible to keep one's eyes closed, to fail to understand that Jesus' kingship is fragile, as it relies only on God, and is expressed in kindness, humility, meekness, compassion, and self-giving. Even today, it is possible to not recognize God's free and forgiving love in his face, especially when we are comfortable in our own self-sufficiency.

At times, we Christians are afraid to open our eyes; we are afraid to accept the sudden manifestations of God who calls us to love our brothers and sisters, and also to forgive them. Even we Christians are afraid to go against the tide, to make gestures of sharing and communion, to open our hearts to the service of others, to make strong evangelical choices. And today, at the international level, many are afraid to make choices that lead to true peace.

In some cases, this fear of the "other" gradually becomes a blind and absurd hatred, as in all kinds of terrorism that cause bloodshed in our world. And yet, at the core of the Gospel, there is no darkness. Rather, there is a consoling and radiant, serene scene, full of joy and hope: the light of salvation emanating from the Child Jesus. There is Mary, whose love can see the Lord's presence even in the darkest nights of history.

Thus, in this episode of the Gospel, we are confronted by two kinds of logic: Herod's and the Magi's. Two types of society stem from these: a society entrenched in the ruthless defense of its own interests (Herod's), and an open society in search of humanity's true good (the Magi's). The second one is the society, or community, that I mentioned in one of my pastoral letters, titled *Restarting from God*, where I call it "an alternative society or community."

Restarting afresh from God is thus the primary

prerequisite, which I also proposed at the very beginning of my journey as bishop of the Church of Milan, with my pastoral letter on the contemplative dimension of life. In this letter, I explained that to start from God means to seek God with insistence and perseverance, just like the Magi: to search for God as the night seeks the dawn. Restarting afresh from God means to live an inner life and transmit to others this holy restlessness of a tireless search for the Father's hidden face, a search that is not content to merely read the Scriptures but wants to delve deeper, to question, to avoid repeating words without understanding their meaning, their essence, their wisdom, and their mystery.

We Christians are also called to reveal to our contemporaries the narrow-mindedness of certain figures who, like Herod, are content with what is lesser than God, anything that can easily become an idol. God is far greater than our hearts, our expectations, and our shortsighted hopes. It is only by delving into the mystery of Jesus that we can experience his revelation in Nazareth, so that the Church can become, in its fullness and its many different analogical realizations, an ideal of communion in the making, intended to show to a fragmented and divided society that thoughtful and genuine relationships, based on the Gospel, can indeed exist; in other words, to show that the primacy of God also means the emergence of the best that there is in the heart of humanity and society.

Returning to the passage from Luke describing Jesus' birth, we learn that while Joseph and Mary are in Bethlehem, her time to give birth comes, as reported in the central verse of the story: "And she gave birth to her firstborn son and wrapped him in bands of cloth, and laid him in a manger, because there was no place for them in the inn" (Luke 2:7). And that is the whole account of Jesus' birth; there is no significant or extraordinary fact: no halo, no radiant scene. All we have is a simple birth account and one small, particular detail: the child is laid in a manger in a stable.

However, this little detail turns out to be a relevant aspect. In fact, the evangelist Luke mentions it again a few verses later, when describing the angel's announcement to the shepherds concerning this child born in the city of David: "This will be a sign for you: you will find a child wrapped in bands of cloth and lying in a manger" (Luke 2:12). Continuing the story, Luke says that the shepherds went with haste to Bethlehem and found Mary and Joseph, and the baby lying in the manger.

We might ask, among many other questions that this story evokes, why the evangelist insists on this small sign. How does this inconspicuous detail in the story illuminate for us readers one of the meanings of this event, which still today is part of our nativity scenes and is always a source of wonder for those who reflect on it carefully? What does this sign mean? It is a simple sign of recognition, with no extraordinary or miraculous quality; rather, it has the character of extreme ordinariness, of absolute poverty. Even for the Bedouins, the shepherds who lived in tents and had no homes, there was pride in having a dwelling place where one could stay away from prying eyes and feel comfortable. But for our family of Nazareth, for this child, there is no such place. Therefore, this circumstance becomes a sign, a way to distinguish him from all the newborns who lived at that time in Bethlehem.

It is a sign that is also a teaching—it is not by chance that the evangelist reiterates it—for not only is it a distinctive sign and recognition of a condition of extreme poverty and deprivation, but also one that belongs to the way Jesus manifests himself to us. In fact, it is first a sign of nonacceptance as the text makes clear: "...and laid him in a manger, because there was no place for them in the inn" (Luke 2:7), or as the evangelist John says: "He came to what was his own, and his own people did not accept him" (1:11). It is the sign of a painful rejection. From the outset, Jesus meets no applause, enthusiasm, or success but only discomfort, troubles, and rejection. He immediately comes in contact with the dark realities of our human existence—even in its simplest expressions, for this very reason—made all the more painful because they occurred in circumstances in which anyone should have the right to a place to be born.

As mentioned earlier, on Christmas Eve, unlike the Roman Rite, in the Ambrosian Rite, we read the Prologue of John's Gospel, which offers a different expressive mode. We no longer hear a simple, almost naïve story, but a theological hymn in the tradition of great religious poetry, rich in concepts: life, light, darkness, acceptance, rejection, the Word that became flesh and lived among us.

Among the rich and evocative words in John's Gospel, it is worth noting two expressions that recall each other. First, "The light shines in the darkness, and the darkness did not overcome it" (1:5); second, in part mentioned earlier: "He came to what was his own, and his own people did not accept him. But to all who received him...he gave power to become children of God" (1:11–12). Here we see side by side the two main attitudes: that of rejection (the darkness that did not comprehend the light) and acceptance (those who receive him).

What does this rejection of the light signify, and what is this deep darkness? In human history and in our experience, we can distinguish three types of darkness.

The easiest to recognize is the darkness represented by the individual offenses that obscure and demean human history, such as aggression, theft, betrayal, dishonesty, infidelity. This is the darkness that clouds the soul of each one who commits these acts, the darkness of our own personal sins.

However, there is also the darkness that might be identified as "social deviance," that is, all forms of disorder that disrupt, damage, and ruin society. Unemployment, economic crisis, widespread corruption, political crises during which we lose sight of the meaning and reasons for communal living, discord, wars: these are all signs of the collapse and laceration of the social fabric that are not due to a single criminal act, but are the index of a common malaise, a contagious disease that corrodes and destroys the body politic. These phenomena can be defined as darkness because they are the result of mistaken attitudes, ignorance, wrong understanding of the process of social living, performed in disregard for the conditions of the development of a community of people. These are sins of the will and darkening of the intelligence, and not just of individual intelligence: they are the result of collective social disorders, of widespread moral, but also mental, indolence.

What is worse than this kind of "social" darkness is a certain type of "cultural" darkness consisting of a mentality, a collective attitude that, having lost the sense of higher values, no longer finds in itself the strength to react and to expose, fight back, and overcome the social deviance mentioned above. This darkness includes the recent opinions about life and death, the meaning of life, and why we are here on earth. It is the loss of hope of an eternal future for humanity; it is the deepest and most unfathomable darkness of all.

Thus, the light is rejected because we refuse the primary principles of acceptance, which are a healthy understanding of both God and humanity: the sense of being creatures, the awareness of our sin and need for salvation.

Against this hopeless darkness, the Christmas Gospel opposes the welcoming of the Word of God: "But to all who received him...he gave power to become children of God." Salvation from darkness comes from the acceptance of the Christmas message, of "making room" for the Savior who is born for us. This is what renews us and illuminates for us the perception of the eternal values and benefits that make human life a worthy life—better still, a life as children of God.

Only the values of faith and hope are able to reconstruct the horizon of meaning even of the more dreadful and desperate human events and allow us to find the strength to prevail over tragedies with our love still intact. It is from reconstructing this horizon of meaning and from the power of love stemming from faith and hope, that we find the energy to recognize and overcome the disruption of the social fabric as well as the strength to confess and atone for our personal mistakes that have contributed to that deterioration. This is the meaning of conversion, the grace of a new life in Christ, the ability to live in this world as children of God: it is Christmas coming into our lives.

Therefore, Jesus was born for all of us: for those who believe and for those who claim not to believe. Jesus was born for those who work, suffer, and hope for a better world and for those who, tired and disappointed, experience confusion and anguish. No one is excluded from the happiness of Christmas. Everyone can accept this new Word, this Word made flesh.

Everyone can open the doors to him, so that, in him, we can become children of God.

Neither wars nor hatred of any kind will ever be able to stop Jesus because he is the one who conquers death with life, hatred with love, falsehood with truth. It depends on us: to follow him, accept witnessing with him to this new order of values, and say to him that yes that he evokes in us.

If, as St. Peter states in Acts 4:12, humanity's only salvation is in Jesus Christ, the Son of God, and if Jesus himself determined that Peter ("You are Peter, and on this rock I will build my church"—Matt 16:18) was to be the first vicar of Christ on earth, then the only authentic way to welcome God, who became man for us, is within the Church.

Having made such a vast claim, we can add to this three other convictions regarding the Church. First, the path of the Church is not smooth, like a well-marked highway, free of obstacles and crossings, which we have to take only once without turning back. It instead passes through houses and fields, close to the reality of people's lives, and is a witness to all the events in our everyday experience. This path runs through the squares and markets, passes in front of banks and stock exchanges, close to barracks and hospitals. In other words, it is not removed from any of the phenomena that occur every day in our streets: encounters and clashes, greetings and insults, happiness, misfortunes and twists of fate, slips, bickering, corruption, and shootings.

Although the path of the Church is peaceful and offers everyone a chance to walk toward a peaceful goal, it cannot avoid passing through problematic places and areas. It is like the road from Jerusalem to Jericho, used by merchants and thieves, priests and Samaritans, known for robberies and injuries, but also acts of kindness: we can run into the Good Samaritan and find the inn of refuge. In short, the path of the Church, of the Christians who are part of the ecclesial community, and of the bishops who walk it, is connected to all the events and sufferings of the people, and is not detached from any of them.

The second conviction derives from the first: the path of the Church is difficult—in the words of the Gospel, it is narrow. Yet, it is not an uncertain path that goes nowhere. It is well-defined, and in another sense, it is broad, with room for everyone. Jesus speaks of a narrow path and a narrow gate that lead to life. This is precisely the path, the door through which everyone must strive to enter with their own personal decisions, matured on the path of the Church, which is welcoming, appealing, inviting, and open to all.

The path of the Church does not want to impose anguish on anyone, but rather wants to enhance, deepen, and validate our freedom. It is not a secondary path for sectarians or initiates, but is meant to help reach fullness of life for all those of good will and those who do not refuse to travel at least part of the road together. The important thing is to avoid going off the road, going astray, despairing or giving up discouraged; we must persevere on the path. The Church is therefore a welcoming, inviting, stimulating path to walk on with joy, always starting from the point where we find ourselves, with the belief that we can always do a little better and a little more.

In the current situation, which is basically one of distrust and fear, the Church does not wish to take the position of those who say, "You are not one of us, you are not with us." Rather, in all its approaches, it is trying to say with Jesus, "You are not far from the kingdom of God; you too can walk part of the road with us."

An example of this attitude is found in the story of the Magi: as their description indicates, they were "sorcerers," that is, astrologers, soothsayers, belonging to a pagan and superstitious culture, therefore, men outside the monotheistic revelation and the pure faith of Israel. Nevertheless, they, not the lawyers, are the ones who set out to follow the star. One could argue that the star was a superstitious sign, related to the world of idolatry, which believed in the influence of the stars on human history. Instead, the star becomes for them a providential sign, a means for the first proclamation of the Gospel. The one who is calling us at the end of this path—the Lord, the Child Jesus in the manger—can see far ahead and knows how to reach us each in our own situation, even if flawed or ambiguous, to get us out of ourselves and put us on the road.

Finally, the third conviction: the path of the Church is difficult to take as it passes through all the sufferings of this world, and yet it remains open, inviting, and welcoming; ultimately it is the path of life as opposed to the path of death. It is taken in faith; it is the path of life and faith that requires and inspires a personal decision. It is not a path that one takes mechanically or by force of inertia, dragged by a crowd but not knowing where one is going, as in certain public events. It is a journey on which each one is called to gradually discover the inner life of their own conscience and make personal decisions that are increasingly more relevant, walking briskly and unswervingly.

Thanks to the path, the human mind that makes room for God's plan becomes awake and agile, capable of developing creative and planning skills. It is led, even in the vicissitudes of this world, by the confidence that God's plan has poured into each of our hearts. The Lord has big plans for us, for human history; plans that have as their point of reference Christ crucified and risen, he who is the brightest and most certain splendor of truth.

On this path of the Church, the bishop is the one who has to sustain this awakening of consciousness, this appropriation of interiority, this awareness of the gift of truth and freedom that the Holy Spirit puts in the heart of everyone undertaking this journey. Therefore, those who set out on this path are not part of an indistinct crowd but rather people ever more conscious of their choices and goals, eager to share with the largest possible number of persons this realization, so that they themselves can make the first step toward self-recognition and leave behind the anonymity and the Babel of languages and opinions to become instead mature and responsible men and women in all their actions.

When all is said and done, this path of a peaceful nation of men and women who are free and conscious is the only hope for a world shaken by conflicts and threats. These are the same people who flock to this path that at times is stained by the blood of martyrs, or is overcast with threatening clouds of terrible conflicts. However, it seems to me that we should always strive to perceive the great light of Jesus in the daily fabric of our ordinary stories. Despite everything, as Christians, we still have the ability to recognize the signs of the Lord even in the darkness and gloom of our days.

Hence, those who are disheartened and give up, or those who think that there are solutions that do not require an increase of consciousness, courage, and faith, will only encounter misery and affliction. Neither in the learned and inquisitorial wavering of the priests of Jerusalem, nor in Herod's rage and retaliations, but in the end, only in the persevering journey of the Magi will we be able to contemplate the light that from the outset shone on their path and gave them the strength to follow it. This light of the Lord, which according to the prophecies of Isaiah (chapter 60) will shine over Jerusalem, over all the earth, defeating the deep darkness and clouds that envelop the nations, will be recognized only by those who, before everything else, accept the humility of Bethlehem, as the Magi did.

In conclusion, I would like to stress that the event of God's incarnation, which we celebrate at Christmas, does not have God as the only protagonist, nor is God's decision to come among us as a man the main story. Of course, God is always first, but God's coming into history necessitates, as a possible condition, the free acceptance of the human creature, represented here by Mary. Mary, who for nine months carried Jesus in her womb, gave birth to him, and laid him in a manger, becomes the symbol and the paradigm of all humanity that freely makes room for God's intervention of grace and loving salvation.

6

You Will Find a Child in the Poverty of a Stable

The section of Luke's Gospel that is read in the churches of the Archdiocese of Milan on Christmas Day is a reflection on the nativity scene and a description of

Jesus' birth. However, this description leaves us surprised. In fact, Jesus never appears in the foreground; he is not described as a child normally is, saying that he is beautiful, lovable, cute, crying, or poor; there is no particular description of him. Yet he is the hero of the story, the person who from this point on will be the main protagonist of the gospel narrative. Any other author would describe the main character from the very start, presenting every aspect, making the readers picture him in their minds.

Instead, this gospel passage speaks of other characters. In the first part, we learn more details about Joseph, Mary, and their journey. The second part describes the shepherds guarding their flock overnight and what happens to them. Within these two scenes, between Joseph and Mary, and the shepherds, is contained Jesus. Jesus as a child is silently, almost imperceptibly, in the midst of everything that moves around him; yet, he is the one who attracts all things to himself.

Jesus as a child is at the center of the action, at the center of the mystery of Joseph and Mary, and at the center of the shepherds' story; he is at the heart of the account of that wonderful night, the meaning of them all. Everything is there with him, everything comes from him, everything leads to him, and he is the silent center of this reality. In the days leading up to Christmas, we prepare nativity scenes. Children prepare them with love, with few or many characters, modestly, solemnly, or artistically. When we contemplate the nativity scene, we can see that it is composed of different characters, but all head toward Jesus, are connected to him, depart from him, or are judged by him, and find their meaning in him.

Jesus is thus at the center of the nativity scene, silent, not described, not praised or admired, but giving meaning to everything manifested around him. He himself is the meaning of all that happens: Joseph goes to Bethlehem where Jesus will be born; Mary accomplishes her wonderful task by giving birth to Jesus, wrapping him in bands of cloth, and laying him in the manger. All her gestures are focused on Jesus. A great light shines in the night upon the shepherds; they set out, go to the place where they find Jesus, and enfold him with their tenderness. Jesus is silent, he cannot speak, walk, or move, and yet they all move and talk around him. Already Jesus' birth anticipates what will take place in the scene of the resurrection, as described by John 20:19, where it says, "Jesus came and stood among them and said, 'Peace be with you.'"

Thus, from the moment of his birth, Jesus comes and lays in the midst of our lives, at the center of all our actions. He is at the center of those who know that they come from him, for him, and around him; but he is also in the middle of those who do not know it. Jesus says to all, "Peace be with you." The nativity scenes that we prepare and that represent our world (many are symbols of everyday reality) all reflect the wars, hunger, suffering, loneliness, and hard work. But it is all to put Jesus at the center, because the Son of God cannot be put aside, away from us, as he is inside every fold of our existence.

This tiny little baby who might seem marginal in the course of the great events of the world is instead an unmistakable sign that, with him and in him, everything in the world that is small, poor, weak, and rejected is important.

Thus, the Gospel puts all that is small, solitary, poor, weak, rejected, and marginalized at the center. We Christians must try to do the same: give center stage in our churches to everything that we are tempted to forget because it is too little, too marginal, too weak to have a voice, too obscure to arouse interest. With Jesus, in the Child Jesus, these realities are precisely what truly matter. From the beginning, Jesus draws the entire world to himself, to his simplicity, humility, and poverty. He draws all with an attraction that will end with the cross and on the cross, from which he will keep drawing all to himself, with an attraction that is perpetuated in the humility of the Eucharist that we celebrate and from which, today, Jesus draws to himself the entire world.

Therefore, we are like the characters in an ideal nativity scene that embrace the universe and whose center is Jesus. We are a bit like the characters who appear around the Lord to pay him homage as active, dynamic, and responsible "extras." Like Mary and Joseph, who worship him, wrap him in bands of cloth, and feed him with care, and like the shepherds who run to greet him, we all want to be among the people of good will who enter the nativity scene and officially recognize Jesus at the center. We want to and must become the protagonists of an evangelical action that turns us into neighbors to others and who, together with Jesus, take as point of reference every weakness, poverty, and vulnerability. Christmas is the litmus test of our Christian truth, if indeed we become neighbors to others in this way.

Jesus' birth and the nativity scene teach us countless, even unusual, lessons about God, because we are accustomed to think of God primarily as great, immense, infinite, omnipotent, and we expect benefits from him. Humanity knew well these attributes of God even before Jesus' birth. Jesus, instead, not only teaches us these realities of God, but does so by combining them with others that we would not immediately expect from or as part of God. For example, the Child Jesus teaches us that God is not only great, inaccessible, immense, and eternal, but also that God came among us and became our "neighbor," not just as a good neighbor who brings gifts but one who shares our needs, our suffering, our loneliness, our exiles, our evictions, our pains, and our poverty.

From the Child Jesus we thus learn that God is not only immensity, but also, in a mysterious way, littleness, as God became a child for us. God is not only the generous giver of gifts, but also kindness, compassion, and solidarity with us in our entire small, weak being. The Child Jesus teaches us that God is not only great, powerful, and wonderful, but also that in God there is something that we cannot define and that in us is called *humility*: to accept the last place, the manger of the beasts where no one would want to lay. The absolute humility of Jesus in the manger reveals unknown qualities of God: the ability to be present in the insignificant and poor as well as the ability to give himself to us without reserve. These are some of the everlasting lessons that we learn from the Child Jesus, because in him are hidden all the treasures of wisdom and knowledge.

Therefore, Christmas is the offer of salvation made to us here and now to the extent that we are able to recognize and accept God's intervention in the salvific form chosen for us: the littleness, insignificance, and poverty of the stable at Bethlehem. God has thus chosen to carry out his plan of salvation, to let us enter into communion with him through littleness and poverty. He came to become flesh, as stated in John's Gospel, to become *man* in all the historical richness of the term, embracing even our condition of weakness, fragility, limitation, and death to redeem us.

The true meaning of the Christmas we celebrate is the mystery of the Son of God, of the Word of God, who assumed for himself our fragile condition as creatures, who came into the world to give us the same life of God. It truly is the wondrous event of our salvation; it is a new creation, and the beginning of our redemption that will be completed later on the cross. With Christmas, our life is truly assumed by God, by the Word made flesh.

At the beginning of the Letter to the Hebrews, which is read during the liturgical celebration of

Christmas Eve, the incarnate Son of God is called "reflection of God's glory and the exact imprint of God's very being" (Heb 1:3). Further, in the Prologue of John's Gospel we read, "And the Word became flesh and lived among us, and we have seen his glory, the glory as of a father's only son, full of grace and truth" (1:14).

It seems counterintuitive that the word *glory* in both the Letter to the Hebrews and in John's Prologue refers to the mystery of a God who became a frail and weak man. Yet, on Christmas night, we are invited to contemplate, in the poor and humble child of Bethlehem, the light and glory of the Word of God, the Son of God. The word *glory* in the Bible indicates the power and splendor with which God's presence is revealed to humanity, but it is a glory that is primarily the power of love, the power of communicating and donating Oneself; the power of becoming humble and low.

This is how every aspect of God's divine greatness is revealed and how God's glory shines. This is why Christmas is somehow a celebration of paradoxes: in the humbling of God's Son, God's glory is revealed; in the weakness of God's Son, God's power is made manifest. This is how God is expressed in Jesus' earthly life, in Jesus' way of living and behavior.

Through God's grace, we proclaim as Christians that in the little things, the greater ones are revealed; in a small host is present the Son of God, in the cup, his blood. In the communion we receive, God comes toward us and embraces us. In the disease that frightens us and causes suffering and death is the merciful presence of the Son of God, who welcomes us and says, "Come with me in my kingdom."

If Christmas is a time of God's manifestation, this manifestation is certainly different from how we usually imagine God, that is, as the one who is in heaven, who is above all, whose transcendence dominates the universe. In fact, God is made manifest as the one who descends, the one who lowers and empties himself. Compared to our classical conception of God, here is the novelty: this God is no longer the supreme being above all, but a God who lowers and empties himself, who becomes little, almost insignificant.

It is true, in our painful experience, we see that our world is often harsh and violent, traumatized by so many seemingly irreconcilable egoisms. Hence, it seems obvious that when God appears among us, we would tend to imagine a severe judge or an outraged ruler who comes to destroy evil, to humiliate and put an end to sinners, to inflict deserved punishment on humanity. Instead, the message of Christmas proclaims that everything is the opposite: God's gratuitous, generous, and forgiving love is revealed to us through God's star, God's only Son, who in turn appears to us as a weak, sweet, and defenseless child in his mother's arms, with the delicateness of the small flickering light coming from Bethlehem. It is a small light, but one that is pure and able to illuminate even our darkest nights. This voiceless child can still speak to each one of us personally, saying, "I love you, I forgive you, I respect you, you're good, you're important to me, I'm giving your life back to you, I need you." This is what God does for us.

As mentioned several times in the Letter to the Hebrews (see 2:5–18; 12:2), Christ, from being equal with God, glorious, and almighty, then emptied, humbled, and almost annihilated himself by taking the form of a poor and insignificant servant. As we worship him at Christmas in the manger as a poor and fragile child, we celebrate the manifestation of a mystery hidden for centuries in the heart of God, a mystery that is revealed with inexplicable yet simple gestures. To quote a contemporary monk, "Against our expectations of the magnitude and power of God, we are told that this power consists precisely in the ability to manifest itself in the vulnerability and exposure to a life as precarious and risky as ours; in offering itself to our poor hands and words; and in becoming recognizable in the fragile yet promising body of a child."

It follows, then, that the divine trait in humanity, and therefore in each one of us, is not so much our ability to transcend ourselves or assert ourselves over others, but rather our ability to lower ourselves, to serve out of love, to become poor with the poor.

7

Renouncing Impiety and Worldly Passions

In the Letter to Titus, the second reading for Christmas Mass in the Ambrosian Rite, St. Paul writes, "For the grace of God has appeared, bringing salvation to all, training us to renounce impiety and worldly passions, and in the present age to live lives that are self-controlled, upright, and godly, while we wait for the blessed hope and the manifestation of the glory of our great God and Savior, Jesus Christ" (2:11–13).

Jesus thus comes to teach us to deny what the apostle calls "worldly passions," that is, the competition to see who can better cheat one's own neighbors and prevail over them, the competition founded on selfishness and fear that our neighbor will take advantage of us first. Jesus comes to teach us, in God's name, a different attitude, an attitude of compassion and *pietas*, that is, "the filial piety," the trusting relationship of children and Father; a relationship that opens the heart and allows us to trust each other.

The effect of this attitude, as stated in St. Paul's Letter to Titus, is that we live lives that are "self-controlled, upright, and godly." Self-control is the opposite of materialism, the craving for new things; it is the ancient and challenging virtue of knowing how to be content. How new these words sound to us in today's world! To be content means that we can live justly so that each receives what is necessary, and that selfishness does not drive one to try to prevail on another. As St. Paul says, Jesus teaches us to live modestly, justly, and compassionately, that is, fully open to relationships of kindness and love. Christmas thus becomes a feast of anticonsumerism, a celebration that finds its true meaning in humility and goodness.

Jesus teaches us this new way of life with his own lowliness as he appears among us as a child. He teaches us this new way of life through the gift of his Spirit that is bestowed upon us. He teaches us this new way of life through the life-giving power of his Word that transforms us. Finally, Jesus teaches us this new way of life through the grace of the sacraments of reconciliation and the Eucharist that we receive, especially at Christmas.

It is a new way of life, a fraternal life, that Jesus reveals to us with his kindness, with his coming as a child among us. St. Paul goes on to say that this new way of life "self-controlled, upright, and godly" is lived in this world "while we wait for the blessed hope and the manifestation of the glory of our great God and Savior, Jesus Christ."

Christ's birth, therefore, teaches us to reject evil and the false knowledge of God in order to open ourselves to the true knowledge of the Father. Christ's birth teaches us to deny worldly passions—power, success, the acquisition of money as the only purpose in life—not to place them over and above human dignity. Instead, Christ's birth teaches us to place them lower, turning them into means and, therefore, to use them only in order to help to serve God and our neighbors, to promote truth, justice, and solidarity, to overcome hunger, to defeat unemployment, and to raise the standard of living, of love, of communion among men and women. This is what Jesus taught us: to live as sons and daughters, brothers and sisters. Jesus reveals to us the truth of our lives and how we should believe and love.

Regarding the Christmas event, we can draw another conclusion that can be formulated thus: if God, in Jesus, has loved us so much that he became like one of us, it follows then, according to Jesus' own words, that whatever we do to one of the least of our brothers and sisters, we do it to him ("just as you did it to one of the least of these who are members of my family, you did it to me"—Matthew 25:40). Whoever has fed, clothed, welcomed one of the least and poorest brothers or sisters, will have fed, welcomed, loved the very Son of God. Whoever has rejected, driven away, forgotten, overlooked one of the smallest and poorest of them, will have rejected, driven away, overlooked the very Son of God. Or, to quote St. John, "Those who say, 'I love God,' and hate their brothers or sisters, are liars; for those who do not love a brother or sister whom they have seen, cannot love God whom they have not seen. The commandment we have from him is this: those who love God must love their brothers and sisters also (1 John 4:20–21)."

Compared to John's elevated and learned tone and style, the story of Jesus' birth in Luke's Gospel draws attention to the ordinary aspects of everyday life: "This will be a sign for you: you will find a child wrapped in bands of cloth and lying in a manger" (2:12). We find ourselves literally thrown into everyday life's simplicity and lowliness, into poverty, because a child wrapped in bands of cloth is not a particularly noteworthy sign. In those days, certainly many children in Bethlehem were born in those months and wrapped in bands of cloth, but the sign in question is primarily a sign of poverty, of a life of suffering: "a child wrapped in bands of cloth and lying in a manger." Of the many children wrapped in bands of cloth, there was only one so poor, with no home, so lacking in everything that he was laid in a manger.

From a sign of rejection, this key to understanding the passage, namely the small detail of the manger—to which the evangelist returns more than once in the chapter—becomes also a sign of judgment.

For Jesus the Savior, born in the city of his ancestor David, the great king, some things are essential and others are not. Jesus searches for and teaches us what really matters. He teaches us that being is more important than having, that there are many things that seem important but, at a closer look, they are less so than others. He teaches us that there are fundamental values that we cannot and must not give up—and these are not the values of possession.

Thus, the detail of the manger is also a sign of poverty, a sign of God's mysterious way of being in history that challenges and frightens us a little. We might ask ourselves the following: What does this poverty of Bethlehem mean? That this poverty of the nativity scene, which on the one hand is the result of neglect and human sin, is on the other hand a concrete, historical sign through which Jesus chose to manifest himself and will continue to use to manifest himself for the rest of his life? How does Jesus' poverty challenge us today? What does it say to the Church? What does it say to each one of us Christians?

Certainly, we can easily grasp the first aspect of this message on the very day of Christmas. Indeed this message is that we are to be on the side of the poor, of all those who need essential aid: shelter, a job, and a meal, or affection, companionship, and health. To be for them, on their side, means to live the preferential option for the poor that is neither privilege nor neglect of one or the other, but care and attention to those who are closer to Christ in the way he chose to come into the world. This is a cultural and operational preference that embraces the whole experience and the way of being Christians: our mentality, our way of working, our social, cultural, and political considerations; it is the fruit of our contemplation of the nativity that drives us to be for the poor, looking for them, recognizing them, helping them, supporting them. How many good deeds the Christian community, by putting itself generously and disinterestedly on the side of those who suffer the most, has accomplished and fulfilled under the inspiration and motivation of the stable of Bethlehem!

But the stable of Bethlehem, with the loving presence of Mary and Joseph, who represent humanity in tender adoration of Jesus, teaches us that it is not enough to just be *for* the poor. If we really want to be with Jesus and grasp the sign of his nativity, we are called to be *with* the poor by putting ourselves in their shoes, entering their suffering, experiencing with them as much as we can, in different ways and different conditions that we need to rediscover and reinvent every day. This means to participate in a communion that should embrace the entire world, since the greater part of humanity is living in poverty, in need, and in a state of underdevelopment. This communion allows us to be *with* all those who suffer and, depending on the different vocations and graces given to the Church by God, inspires us to share in their living conditions, to really understand them, to feel how intolerable it can be, encouraging effective action for development, mutual growth, and connection.

But the sign of Jesus in the manger of Bethlehem takes on a third meaning as well, which is even more difficult for us to accept: we must offer ourselves willingly *for* the poor, for those in need of any kind of help. For instance, consider those who suffer today because of the employment and economic crisis—the entire Christian community must live not only passively, but actively, with strength and creativity, this difficult moment—or all the other poor and suffering people: those who, for whatever reason, need our presence in their lives and whom we must help, especially on Christmas Day.

Yet, perhaps it is not too difficult for us to understand how and why we should be *for* the poor; and we may also understand the reason to be *with* them.

However, what we find more difficult to understand in today's society is what it means to "become poor ourselves." At times we hear this idea in sermons or read it in the Gospel, and it seems to us very far from our society, which requires a high rate of production and consumption in order to be itself. Therefore, it seems that to break with this way of measuring society, and to go beyond these conventionally adopted measurements, is not even worth mentioning anymore.

It is precisely for this reason that we need to stop before the stable of Bethlehem and reflect for a moment on what it means to "become poor ourselves," to grasp the profound meaning of poverty in the gospel message, which ultimately means freedom. In fact, this message conveys an inner detachment and freedom with regard to our assets and belongings that are so important to us, not only our economic assets, but also cultural ones, our professional qualities, our time, and our physical strength. We thank God for what has been given to us, but we should also ask God to help us become inwardly detached so that we may be able to share these assets with others, to do so lovingly, and even to learn to deny ourselves, if necessary, to give to others, to enrich the poor, the last, the voiceless; in short, to give so that we may attain equality and a living sign of unity.

The Lord puts these things in our hearts: God makes us understand how difficult it is, but also how liberating. The Lord makes us understand the ability to exorcise the ghost of a mechanized society that is reduced to a specific mass and number; to grasp, in the sense of detachment and freedom of the heart, the victory of the human spirit over the forces of disintegration; and finally, to grasp the cosmic sign for the world of today represented by this baby wrapped in bands of cloth and lying in a manger.

8

This Grace of Salvation Is for All

In the Letter to Titus, which is read during the liturgical celebration on Christmas Day in the Ambrosian Rite, Paul announces that "the grace of God has appeared, bringing salvation to all" (Titus 2:11). These words are a synopsis, a brief summary of the cosmic, universal, and salvific meanings that the event of Jesus' birth assumes for each of us today. In fact, Christmas has a universal quality: Jesus was born to announce to all, without exception, that the Father loves us to the point of giving us his Son, to make us become like him, children of God.

The messianic mission of this child is widened to include all humanity, and Christmas, this descent of God in poverty and peace, is only the beginning of what, through the cross and Easter, will reach people of all races and colors, religious and cultural traditions, regardless of human and social distances. Christmas thus touches us deeply as a commitment to the dignity of all, as a commitment to promote this dignity that, two thousand years ago, God came to promote by becoming a man, a child for us.

The fundamental aspect of the Christmas feast is this universality, this reaching of all. The shepherds who ran to the stable are only the first in an endless procession that we ourselves now join, one that will include all the peoples of the earth, from the East and West, North and South. We should not be surprised if in this procession we find ourselves walking, not only with people we know, of our own race and culture, but also with people of different languages, color, nationality, and culture, all attracted by the light of the stable from which the message of peace in justice descends.

We should look around and recognize these brothers and sisters who, perhaps without knowing it, are attracted to this stable from far away, because I think that the future destiny of Europe—a multiracial society and civilization—will be precisely to unite around the manger and the Christmas tree all people reconciled in the sign of the peace and justice that come from the Lord. If this dream seems too hypothetical and distant, let us repeat the words of Isaiah, "The zeal of the LORD of hosts will do this" (Isa 9:7).

In other words, while Christmas is the celebration of the event itself, the Epiphany is the fulfillment, as it were, of Christmas for us, the yes of the Gentile world that rushes toward Jesus born in Bethlehem: the Epiphany is the feast of our faith and the universality of salvation. As such, it is a missionary feast and this characteristic derives from the universality of God's gift, the missionary and ecumenical character of this gift.

On this feast, therefore, we proclaim that the coming of Jesus is for everyone. It wants to reach everyone, and it is missionary in spirit. The Magi, in fact, are considered the first representatives of distant peoples called to faith, the first who set out in search of the God who saves. It is not out of place to say, in this sense, that the Epiphany is the feast of humanity's pilgrimage in this life to search for God. It is the feast of every man and woman who, having sought God, find him, and having found him, still seek him, as do the rest of us. Ours is a pilgrimage carried out with patience, perseverance, starting over every day, through many pitfalls, just like the Magi, while letting the star guide us and overcoming all the difficulties that we encounter along the way, whether caused by other people or our surroundings.

A fundamental component of the feast of the Epiphany is this missionary or ecumenical dimension, which is global and reaches every corner of the inhabited earth. This dimension is particularly present in the liturgical celebration of the Epiphany according to the Ambrosian Rite: the first prayer states that all peoples are called to salvation. Then the first reading, from the wonderful prophecy of Isaiah 60:3, proclaims that "nations shall come to your light." The second reading, from Paul's Letter to the Ephesians, proclaims that "the Gentiles," that is, pagans, the non-Jews, those who were not the people of the covenant and could therefore be considered second class citizens, almost inferior with regard to the divine promise, are also called to participate fully in the same inheritance of the children of God: "So then you are no longer strangers and aliens, but you are citizens with the saints and also members of the household of God" (2:19). Every man and woman, therefore, without exception, is called to participate in the gifts of God, which come from the divine initiative of salvation, and to form one body, together with the Jews and with all other peoples, in Jesus, who loves us and gives himself to us.

Together with this message addressed to all peoples, the Letter to the Ephesians also reveals Paul's awareness of proclaiming the mystery of the Gentiles' call to the faith. For Paul it was an important event that marked his entire life, an event shared by every Christian called to evangelize, and especially by every priest and bishop who, with Paul, is called to this same mission and awareness. All believers are called to bear courageous witness to their faith in every moment of life. This testimony stems from the belief that the message of the Gospel—that is, God's plan—is for all people, is good for everyone, and is a message of salvation, liberation, and hope for all.

We all make this commitment with regard to Christmas. This is the fullness that Christmas wants to spread, not only in the heart of each of us, of our families, of our personal lives, but also in the heart of all the cultural commitments of our society, so that we see the prophecy of consolation and hope that the Prophet Isaiah announced to a suffering and divided city fulfilled for us as well. This hope, the same evangelical hope, is the strength of this announcement that helps us to live, even and especially in times of moral and sociopolitical crisis, when the temptations of escape are many. But the strength of this plan of God, understood in faith, allows us to see the necessary reference points so that, even in times of crisis, we can spread the seeds of evangelical hope. Why not let the joy of this announcement and the enthusiasm it inspires shine through us?

Like those who went out from Jerusalem and into the desert, where they received John's baptism and acknowledged God's primacy, thus opening themselves to the plan of Jesus' salvation, we also, by leaving behind our private comforts and becoming more socially engaged, make God's plan of salvation possible, evident, and efficacious—a plan that, even now, promises consolation, reassurance, and hope in our everyday lives.

Finally, in the Gospel reading, the apostle Matthew invites us to rejoice with the Magi as we find our inner star to contemplate and worship Jesus, the center of our life and history. Matthew also invites us to rejoice when we are given the occasion to bear witness to Jesus' love and to accompany someone else in crossing the threshold of faith.

Through the narratives of the different readings, the liturgy proclaims Jesus Savior of all men and women, excluding no one. The Church assures us that the child worshipped by the shepherds of Bethlehem is the hope not only of Israel but of all nations, represented in particular by the Magi who come from the East. As mentioned earlier, Paul proclaims that everyone, without distinction, is called in Christ Jesus to participate in the same heritage, as members of the same body and partakers of the divine promises. We could then say, in more contemporary language, that the message of the Epiphany is the universalism of faith and salvation. We could say that this message expresses, as John Paul II said, the globalization of solidarity, meaning that God works in order to make all of humanity a big family, a family of families of people where all are brothers and sisters, so that everyone feels loved, and is saved and redeemed by the blood of the Father's Son, Jesus.

A further point concerns the nature of this testament, of this word of the Scriptures that guarantees the uniformity of the call to all men and women, which is a tangible sign of the universality of the Christian message: what is the more vibrant, immediate, and real sign that continually reminds us of the universality of the Christian message, that is, the nonexistence of different levels among men, but the uniformity of their call and their full belonging to each other, and the full right of everyone to be considered my brother and sister? This tangible sign, this testament that puts us all together on the same level, is the Eucharist. The Eucharist is Jesus, who gave up his life for all equally, calling everyone to participate in his body and his blood, calling those near and far, the shepherds and the Magi from the East. All have an equal right to participate and be called: the Eucharist is the table around which there is harmony of races and peoples, the Eucharist is the crossroads of dialogue where all are called to speak, to express themselves, and to be understood by each other.

During a trip to Israel, on January 6, 1964, from the stable of Bethlehem, Pope Paul VI addressed all those who watch Christianity from the outside, who are, or feel, almost as if they are outsiders: "We wish to work for the good of the world, for its real interest, for its salvation. Indeed, we think that the salvation that we offer is necessary. Christianity's mission is one of friendship between the peoples of the earth; a mission of understanding, encouragement, promotion, and elevation." With these words, Paul VI paraphrased the first verses of chapter 60 of the Prophet Isaiah: the image of light from Jerusalem shines in favor of all nations.

9
The Happiest Wish

In Luke's Gospel, a choir of angels sings to the astonished shepherds, "Glory to God in the highest heaven, / and on earth peace among those whom he favors!" (2:14). With this song, the multitude of the heavenly host announces to us that when we experience God's greatness, immensity, truth, and love, and when we contemplate God born for us in Jesus of Nazareth, not only does it give us great clarity about ourselves, but also the ability to love each other.

In the Scriptures, peace is the fullness of all gifts, the ability of men to share and communicate with each other. I have always insisted on this fundamental aspect of human life and society. I have also often tried to explain the relationship between communication and society, the importance of communicating properly as well as the importance of overcoming the situations where communication breaks down, especially with our brothers and sisters who are sick or handicapped. There is a strong need to start a friendly and affectionate dialogue with them. "Peace among those whom he favors," is the foundation of friendly communication among us, the ability to build a society in which we become transparent to each other and truly recognize ourselves as brothers and sisters. This ideal of peace originates from God.

Peace, in practical terms, means the end of oppressive power structures, liberation from unjust systems. This happens at Christmas through a child, a son, a descendant of David who will create a society of peace and justice. If this is the true meaning of

Christmas, it is therefore impossible to genuinely experience Christmas without heeding and committing ourselves to this message.

A Christmas message that does not speak of peace would betray the sense of this feast, as would a Christmas message that does not speak of justice.

The Gospel makes clear that the prophecy in chapter 9 of the Book of Isaiah is fulfilled in Bethlehem, in Jesus; above him, the angels sing, "On earth peace among those whom he favors!" But it is useful to focus on one aspect of this event and wonder who the one is through whom this prophecy of peace in justice is fulfilled. Is it a great king, a great statesman, a philosopher, a legislator, a leader of armies? The answer is no. As already proclaimed by Isaiah ("A child has been born for us"—9:6), even the Gospel says that it is a child, a child born for us, and the angels do the same: "To you is born this day…a Savior….you will find a child…" (Luke 2:11, 12); a poor child, lying in a manger, rejected by all and marginalized. The splendor of the heavenly host reveals itself precisely above the poverty of the world.

Therefore the Son of God who comes has nothing to do with the imperialist management of peace, a peace imposed by force: as a child, he teaches us that one power cannot be oppressed or suppressed by another power. War cannot end war; we cannot eliminate violence with violence. The glory of God is manifested through peace for all humanity: not a peace imposed from outside and defended with weapons, rather, the peace of Christmas, a peace that comes from within, from accepting Jesus, Prince of Peace, a peace that is harmony between humanity and God, between humanity and the universe, between men and women, and among every fellow human being.

To experience this peace, we must first praise and worship God, give God first place, recognize God's primacy as Mary, Joseph, and the shepherds did. We must accept Jesus in his mystery of littleness, poverty, and humility. This inner peace, this peace of the heart, which we all need, is the fruit of faith: believing that Jesus was born today, for me, for you, and for all. In this sense, the peace of the world depends on each one of us: it depends on me, on my faith in the Lord, who saves us and brings peace through men and women who guard and promote reconciliation day by day.

Although we are familiar with these principles, today we find ourselves confronted with dramas of conscience because it is always tempting to shape society and politics with power, power that subdues power, violence that banishes violence. It is tempting to believe once again in the inevitability and the permanence on earth of war and bloodshed. We are still not convinced, despite proclaiming the contrary on many occasions, that war must not be the means to settle conflicts between nations, and that it should instead be replaced by dialogue and peace negotiations and initiatives.

Christmas comes to us with this demanding message. The mystery of Christmas calls us to a new style of life; it invites us to create an alternative society, a different community, in which relationships are no longer based on competitiveness or conflict, but on charity, forgiveness, and love founded on the Gospel. Do we really believe in these values? Christmas offers an alternative to "violence against violence"; it offers the alternative of the Prophet Isaiah, who is convinced that oppression and war can cease, and speaks of harmony between those who have always been enemies ("The wolf shall live with the lamb"—Isa 11:6). Christmas offers the alternative of Bethlehem and its message that the one who will bring about the miracle of peace is not one who will sit on a throne or mesmerize a crowd, but a simple and poor child. This miracle will not take place by force of arms or persuasion of the media, which seeks to create opinion from the top down, but with "the zeal of the LORD of hosts" (Isa 9:7), through the power of the Holy Spirit, which will be poured out upon all those who open their arms and hearts, filling them with the gifts of peace and joy.

This peace and joy were certainly in peril at the time of Jesus' birth, as for him there was no room in the inn; his birth was in poverty, a prelude to the cross. It reminds me of a poem by Salvatore Quasimodo titled "Natale" (Christmas); we can almost imagine the poet before the nativity scene saying,

> Christmas. I look at the carved nativity scene
> where I see the shepherds who have just arrived
> at the poor stable of Bethlehem.
> Even the Magi in long robes
> greet the powerful King of the world.

But after this simple and peaceful contemplation, the poet, and with him all of us, starts reflecting on life today and makes a bitter observation: "Peace in the heart of Christ forever; / But there is no peace in the heart of men." He continues, asking, "But is there anyone who listens to the child's cry / who will one day die on the cross between two thieves?" Therefore, even in the Child Jesus there is more than just peace: he cries, like all other children in the world, and in his crying is not only the symbol of his future passion, but of all the suffering of all children and adults.

Therefore, God's gifts of this joy and peace do not protect us from suffering and hardships, but are the grace to pass through the evils of the world, carrying Jesus' message of love, overcoming evil with good. This is the hope of Christmas. Anyone can try to overcome evil with evil, but only one, God, is able to promise to overcome evil with good. This is the hope that comes from Jesus.

Between Christmas Day and the Epiphany, on January 1, the Church celebrates the World Day of Peace established by Pope Paul VI in 1968. During one of these celebrations, Pope John Paul II proclaimed, "There is no peace without justice and no justice without forgiveness." The theme of the close relationship between justice and forgiveness is certainly crucial. Even today we feel a strong need for peace, a peace that seems humanly impossible, but which we all—even those who are fighting—want and aspire to. We want the peace that reflects heavenly peace: a peace that arises from healthy relationships with God, with others, with ourselves; a peace that is the only solution to wars; a peace that originates first from our hearts, where the Holy Spirit breathes; a peace that from our hearts should be spread to families, communities, parishes, work places, and therefore, society as a whole. We are called to overcome every conflict and every division through constant reconciliation, "seventy times seven," and sowing gestures of peace.

As Pope John Paul II said in his heartfelt message on that occasion, the great pillars of peace are justice first, and then the love that is forgiveness. It takes great courage to pronounce this word today, but we must also explain that forgiveness is not opposed to justice, but rather to resentment and revenge. It seeks the fullness of justice because it is much more than a fragile and temporary cessation of hostilities. Forgiveness heals deep inside the wounds that gnaw at the human heart.

What, then, does this forgiveness mean and what does it entail? John Paul II reminds us that forgiveness has its origins in each of our hearts. Before being a social reality, it is a personal choice, a choice of our hearts to go against the natural instinct to repay evil with evil, and that has God's love as its example. In fact, God forgives us despite our sins, and Jesus on the cross prays for God to forgive those who have crucified him. This is the measure and the root of all forgiveness.

Of course, this divine measure of forgiveness does not mean that we cannot grasp its value in light of human considerations. When I commit evil, I always hope that others are indulgent, or do not want revenge and will eventually forgive me. Why then should I not try to forgive those who hurt me? Once this becomes clear, we realize that forgiveness is primarily an initiative of the individual, with a social dimension, because we need forgiveness within groups, nation states, the international community. We know that the ability to forgive, to start over, to put the past behind us is the basis of every attempt to build a future society that is more just and caring. But the failure to forgive, especially when this prolongs conflicts, is extremely costly. Instead of using resources for the needs and development of the people, especially the poorest, they are used for war and weapons. If, therefore, we need peace for development, it is also possible only through forgiveness.

As John Paul II said that day, forgiveness is particularly necessary to end the tragic situation in the Holy Land, the place of the life, death, and resurrection of Jesus, Prince of Peace. If there is peace, it will be because there is peace in Jerusalem; and, conversely, if there are still wars, it will be because there are still wars and conflicts that threaten Jerusalem. For this reason, we always keep our eyes fixed on this holy place, which also recalls Christmas, because it is there, in Bethlehem, just a stone's throw away from Jerusalem, that Jesus was born. For this reason, the issue of peace, even the political peace in Jerusalem, has a significance that goes beyond the limits of a specific place. Jerusalem is a universal symbol, and peace there—a peace that we must wish for wholeheartedly and always—is a symbol of peace among all peoples. We strongly urge with renewed emphasis the need to resolve all conflicts, hoping for a new era of mutual respect and constructive solidarity.

The urgency of peace becomes a call to the specific responsibilities of the Christian confessions and of the other great religions to teach, together as we all should, the greatness and dignity of the human person, and to spread greater awareness of the unity of the human race. This is a precise field of both ecumenical and interfaith dialogue and collaboration.

In this regard, Cardinal Ildebrando Schuster, former archbishop of Milan, provided food for thought when, in a homily on Christmas celebrated in Milan's cathedral, he stated, "Today we announce the first page of the Gospel, *Gloria in excelsis Deo et pax on earth hominibus bonae voluntatis."* Peace, he added, "is unity in diversity; just as in the natural world it stems from truth, so did God, in creating different peoples, assign to each different lands, languages, and missions, so that the variety of nations would confer the common good. Proof of this supernatural unity, of this universal peace, is the Gospel, announced to all, without distinction."

Stressing the importance of Christian forgiveness, John Paul II also shared these words of wisdom on the World Day of Peace, "The help that religions can give to peace and against terrorism consists precisely in their *teaching forgiveness*, for those who forgive and seek forgiveness know that there is a higher Truth, and that by accepting that Truth they can transcend themselves."* For this reason, prayer for peace comes before any commitment to peace, because to pray for peace means to open the human heart to the sudden appearance of God's renewing power; to the power of the spirit of the risen Christ; and to the divine grace that can create openings and hope for peace even where it seems that there are only obstacles and closures. To pray for peace means to pray for God's

---
* Message of John Paul II for the celebration of the World Day of Peace, January 1, 2002, http://www.vatican.va/holy_father/john_paul_ii/messages /peace/documents/hf_jp-ii_mes_20011211_xxxv-world-day-for-peace _en.html.

forgiveness and, at the same time, to grow in the courage needed for those who in turn want to forgive wrongs suffered, as we ask in the Our Father, "Forgive us our trespasses, as we forgive those who trespass against us."

10
The Beginning of
All Our Beginnings

The Son of God is born. Our acceptance of this truth ultimately changes everything and gives a new and different light to every moment we live. If God is truly man, if God became man, then this reality cannot but touch the lives of every man and woman, everywhere and always, for God is always, God is everywhere, God is even now, God is here now. The birth of Jesus, the Son of God, in history touches every moment of history, and in particular, touches every Christmas.

Every Christmas we are touched by this event, just as our fathers and mothers were, just as St. Charles Borromeo was when, as he celebrated the last Christmas of his life, just before his death, he cried out to all those who were with him in Milan's cathedral that day, "I announce to you…that the Son of God is born for you. For you! For you he gave his life and for you he died." We Christians today proclaim this message with the same certainty and force that St. Charles did. The Church is touched by the birth of the Son of God, and that is why, on the night of Christmas, it sings as a mother whose son was born; as a child who welcomes a new brother or sister at home; as a bride for the groom; as those singing to the ones that fill their lives; so does the Church sing for the coming of Christ who fills our lives with every richness.

On Christmas Eve, the Church and all of us sing the birth of the Son of God who is our life, who changes our lives, who touches each moment of our experience that we bring along with us at Holy Mass: our poverty, our sins, our sorrows, our intentions, and our desires. This birth is indeed an event that touches each one of us in our daily struggles. It places Jesus between us and our problems. It places Jesus in us to look with new hearts at our problems, all of which have a common denominator: the tear in the human fabric—human suffering. All our struggles, all sorts of struggles, are signs of this tear, the causes of this tear, and signs of either an order that does not yet exist, or of faulty human relationships.

But if Jesus is among us, if God is with us, it is to mend this torn human fabric, to reassemble a genuine human fabric. Jesus is in us to help us live with humanity and dignity, to open our hearts, enlighten our intelligence, so that we can reconstruct this torn and divided human fabric. John's words ("And the Word became flesh") announces the return of humanity to God. With Christmas begins the process of restoring unity: the Son of God comes into the darkness of the world, in the darkness of our internal and external ruins to rebuild the unity between God and humanity, to restore unity within every man and woman, within human society, mending our divisions and putting an end to the conflicts and wars.

It is up to us Christians to readily accept this Christmas message of salvation and unity. It is up to us to welcome Christ on behalf of all humanity and the whole world. It is up to us to believe and hope for those who have lost their faith and hope—in the certainty that the Word of the Lord comes true and will come true, in the certainty that Christmas puts a mysterious seed of new life in the heart of every man and woman that, in due time, will bear fruit. We ourselves are called to set out for Bethlehem, to cherish this great event that is in our midst.

To use the expression "in our midst" means to believe that Christ is born for us now in the Eucharist, in the Word, in the grace of the Holy Spirit: the Child Jesus in our hearts, in our families, and in our Church. In our cities, in our Western world, restless, hopeful, and looking for a new kind of freedom of expression, a new unity among nations, and a new peace, comes this word of hope: "To you is born this day…a Savior, who is the Messiah, the Lord" (Luke 2:11). Christmas is a day made special and holy by a sacred mystery, the mystery of Jesus, the Son of God, who is born for us and is born today. The Church rejoices and we rejoice with the Church, while the angels descend to announce not only an ancient event that took place two thousand years ago, but an event that happens even now, because today the Father makes all things new in the infant Christ, the Son. God is a fire of love that comes down from heaven and becomes little, in Jesus, to be our life, our truth, our way.

Only from this knowledge can our prayer ascend, just like the one that Cardinal Stefan Wyszyński wrote in captivity, "I want to thank you because you exist; because you are the Word; because you are the Son of the Father; because you wanted to become man in the Virgin's womb; because you wanted to lie in the manger of Bethlehem; because you wanted to manifest yourself to the shepherds and the Magi. Let me keep my gaze fixed upon you, follow you step by step. Watch over me, so I may only think about you when you walk into my house."

11
God with Us

Luke's Gospel read on Christmas Day announces a sign of this new life, this new way of being visited by Jesus. At first glance, this sign appears odd, irrelevant: "This will be a sign for you: you will find a child wrapped in bands of cloth and lying in a manger" (2:12). One wonders, why should this be a sign? An event of such immense importance that it involves heaven and earth, angels and humanity: Why then is this sign so simple? A child, wrapped in bands of cloth and lying in a manger.

Certainly, there is in this sign a reference to the immediately preceding text, that is, how and where Jesus was born, "And she gave birth to her firstborn son and wrapped him in bands of cloth, and laid him in a manger, because there was no place for them in the inn" (2:7). This is how Jesus was born, and this is how the shepherds had to find him. But why the emphasis on this sign: wrapped in bands of cloth and lying in a manger? The delicacy of expression, the simplicity of the words, capture a sharp contrast: a child wrapped in bands of cloth—a child who is welcomed with love, cared for, desired, and received with all affection by Mary. True, wrapped in bands of cloth, yet lying in a manger where no child should ever lay because there is no home to welcome him. The child is poor, excluded, rejected.

This contrast between Mary's attention and love and Jesus' poverty and loneliness is the sign that God is present in our world: in the sign of love and affection, and in the sign of poverty. God is present in the sign of love; hence, we are loved. God asks for our love and for our hearts and to be welcomed in our lives. If we contemplate the Child Jesus this way, the holy night of Christmas truly becomes the night of the discovery of God's love, God's mercy, of God who wants to live in communion with us.

The meaning of the presence of Jesus in our midst is that God is with us, God has always been with us, God is in our history. In the pain of our history, God is present, has always been present, and on Christmas night, God is present in Jesus. Emmanuel, "God is with us," is indeed here with us, among us, to give us the certainty that God's love has not abandoned this universe, but is part of it and part of our suffering and pain to bring us, with him, into the fullness of life of the Father. For this reason, Christmas is only the first step of a plan of love and redemption that is not yet fully accomplished because it awaits completion at the end of time. Christmas is when we can contemplate, with the eyes of the flesh and in our historical reality, the true image of God, the image in which humanity was created from the very beginning: this image is Jesus, the son of man and the Son of God.

Another, perhaps more theoretical, facet of the meaning of Jesus' presence in our midst is revealed by John in his first letter: "And we know that the Son of

God has come and has given us understanding so that we may know him who is true" (5:20). This means that, through Jesus, who comes and dwells among us, we receive the understanding to know the true God; we can penetrate the mystery of truth, life, and love. As we penetrate this mystery, through Jesus who is among us, we penetrate the mystery of our being because we are life made for truth and love. All our being corresponds to our deepest desire for truth, love, and life. Thus, we can truly know ourselves, who we are, what we are made for when we know the true God, who is life, truth, and love. The extraordinary truth is that we cannot know God through speculation and assumptions, but by simply looking at Jesus, looking at Jesus becoming man for us, looking at God's life, love, and truth manifested in the life, truth, and love of Jesus. By revealing who God is, Christmas reveals our true being, who we are, what we are called to, what are the fundamental roots of our existence. Those roots are the basis of all our doing, our functioning, our working, our possessing.

From the moment of Jesus' birth, the Gospel introduces us to his humanity so he may become the object of our memory, our thinking, our imagination because through the contemplation of Jesus the Lord, we may know the unknowable, see the invisible, imagine the unimaginable. To look for other knowledge of God than this, the flesh of Jesus made man, means to dangerously play with fantasy, to risk falling into idolatry and, perhaps, to accept a false god, or to know a god that does not lead to the truth of the God of Jesus. All the lessons we might draw from the Child Jesus in Nazareth are therefore the gateway to the knowledge of God. Only by looking at him, contemplating him, will we learn to reject godless ways—that is, all the false ideas of God: a God that is not Father, not love, not mercy, and not with us.

The second and the third readings for the liturgical celebration of Christmas Eve, from the Letter to the Hebrews and John's Gospel respectively, use apocalyptic language: the language of the final revelation of God in the Son, the language of the eternal Word who became flesh and dwelt among us. Nevertheless, we should try to get to the meaning of these difficult concepts, first by asking ourselves what could the expression, "And the Word became flesh and lived among us," mean to our imagination and our hearts. These words are at the heart of the Gospel and sum up in their brevity the whole mystery of Christmas.

Let us focus on a few pages of the Gospel that present more concrete scenarios: Jesus weeping at the tomb of his friend Lazarus; Jesus blessing children brought to him; Jesus tenderly watching the rich young man who asks him what to do to inherit eternal life; Jesus thanking God for revealing hidden truths to infants; Jesus who is indignant against the rigidity of the hypocrites; Jesus who is overcome by sadness in the Garden; Jesus who lets himself be nailed to the cross and die in solitude. Looking back on these and other episodes in the Gospels, we can say that the mystery of God is revealed in tears and weeping; the Divine is expressed in caresses and tenderness; the Absolute becomes exultation and jubilation; the Holy One becomes indignation and anger; the Inaccessible assumes the role of sadness and pain; the Transcendent takes the form of weakness; the Almighty takes on death in solitude. All this among us, for us, in our midst.

When we recall so many episodes in the Gospels that speak of Jesus' tears, blessings, tenderness, joy, indignation, and sadness, and apply them to the transcendent and ineffable mystery of God, perhaps then we will understand a little better what is behind the words of John's Gospel: "And the Word became flesh." Then we will understand something of the meaning of Christmas, that is, the presence of the Divine in the concrete history of a man; the presence of the mystery of God-among-us; the mystery of God who takes upon himself our everyday weaknesses, who shares our life, often weary and fatigued, and enters the mystery of our suffering and our death.

This presence and sharing of our reality and our lives on the part of God did not occur just once, two thousand years ago. This presence and sharing continues and is manifested today, on Christmas night. For Jesus, Son of God and the Word of the Father, becomes forgiveness through the words of absolution of the Church in the sacrament of reconciliation; Jesus speaks through the words of the Mass; Jesus becomes food in the hands of the priest consecrating the bread of the Eucharist; Jesus comes as food and as a friend in our hearts. God wants to fully enter into our fatigued and clouded humanity; God wants us to share in his divine energy, which passes through all time, penetrates our own time, and makes us live, right here and now, the beginning of the fullness of eternal life.

Therefore, this is the true meaning of the words of John's Gospel: "And the Word became flesh and lived among us, and we have seen his glory." This glory has been revealed to us in the simplicity of the nativity scene; it has been contemplated in the love of the Crucified One; it has erupted in the glory of the Risen

One; it is present in the Eucharist under the veil of the sacrament. And the Word became flesh, God became man, lived among us, and dwells in our midst. The Word became a member of the human family; the Word became a child, a man who died, rose again, and has become a living presence in each of us. What is asked of us is simply to recognize that presence, opening our arms to Jesus' coming.

Then every Christmas is a new Christmas; a new gift of friendship and sharing that God makes to every human person and to each of us. On our part, then, every welcoming gesture and then every act of justice, forgiveness, understanding, and solidarity is the natural culmination of the celebration of Christmas.

On Christmas night, let us entrust our intercessions, prayers, and wishes to Mary, the Mother of Jesus. In adoring silence, Mary contemplates the face of the Word who took flesh from her, and in him, she contemplates the face of all men and women on earth, especially those who suffer in body and spirit.